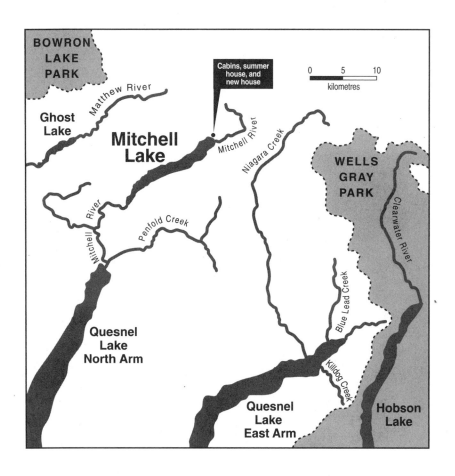

BOWRON
LAKE
PARK

Cabins, summer
house, and
new house

0   5   10
kilometres

Ghost
Lake

Matthew River

Mitchell
Lake

Mitchell River

Niagara Creek

WELLS
GRAY
PARK

Clearwater River

Mitchell River

Penfold Creek

Blue Lead Creek

Quesnel
Lake
North Arm

Quesnel
Lake
East Arm

Killdog Creek

Hobson
Lake

Front cover photo:
Mitchell Lake, looking east
Photo by Vance Hanna

Wm. R. Corbett

Adventures
at Mitchell Lake

Retreating and Recharging in
Canada's Wilderness

Oct. 1/99 : Elder-h g. at FCJ

Here's to you Glenna
for venturing west from
Tronno to Cal-gary.

Best wishes

Bill Corbett

Gordon Soules Book Publishers Ltd.
West Vancouver, Canada
Seattle, U.S.

Canadian Cataloguing in Publication Data
Corbett, William R., 1925-
    Adventures at Mitchell Lake

    ISBN 0-919574-92-0

    1. Corbett, William R., 1925- 2. Mitchell Lake (Cariboo, B.C.)
3. Outdoor life—British Columbia—Mitchell Lake
(Cariboo) I. Title
FC3845.M57C67 1994   971.1'7504'092   C95-910062-8
F1089.M57C67 1994

Published in Canada by
Gordon Soules Book Publishers Ltd.
1352-B Marine Drive
West Vancouver, BC V7T 1B5

Published in the United States by
Gordon Soules Book Publishers Ltd.
620—1916 Pike Place
Seattle, WA 98101

Copy edited by Anne Norman
Designed by Harry Bardal
Typeset by A.R. CompuType Graphics, Vancouver, BC, Canada
Printed and bound in Canada by Hignell Printing Ltd.

CONTENTS

Remembering my Dad and his four brothers—
they knew about retreats.

PREFACE

This is the story of a lake and its impact on my life. Located high in the Cariboo Mountains of British Columbia, Mitchell Lake is still a pristine gem, unexploited and unpolluted. In 1975, I unexpectedly acquired a half share in twenty-four acres at the east end of Mitchell Lake. With the help of fellow outdoor dabblers, I proceeded to build a primitive fishing camp, later developing it into a more comfortable retreat. This has transpired with minimal forethought and planning—it just seemed a good thing to do.

Along with the good fishing and good companionship, I have also experienced hellish, rain-besotted, hard times. I have grown in many ways: environmental awareness, the ability to improvise and create, and the capacity to appreciate the qualities of people different from myself. And I have gained invaluable self-knowledge.

What pushes a person to venture into the wilderness for recreation? For me there has been a therapeutic value in alternating the frustration and stress typical of city life with the exhilaration and immediacy of the wilderness, where exertion—mental as well as physical—produces direct and satisfying results.

Just as this book is going to press, the British Columbia government has announced that the Mitchell Lake area has been designated a protected wilderness. I must acknowledge the dedicated and relentless effort of Doug Radies and Ocean Hellman, who have spearheaded this conservation campaign. May their success be sustained and extended to other areas so that the wilderness experience can be enjoyed by our progeny.

W.R.C. —Oct. 31, 1994

CHAPTER ONE

Where on Earth Is Mitchell Lake?

"I've got bad news and good news," Fred Brooks, my brother-in-law, reported. "That money you gave me to invest in Charolais cattle—well, a Hereford bull got into the act and messed up the works." He was referring to one of his several projects (this one at his Anahim Lake ranch) and to the difficulty of being at the right place at the critical time.

"Anyhow," he continued, "since I guaranteed your investment, I'll give you a half interest in a property I have just acquired in a swap with a neighbor at Anahim. It's at the east end of Mitchell Lake."

"That's interesting," I replied. "But where on earth is Mitchell Lake?" A fateful question, indeed.

"It's in the Cariboo Mountains," he explained. "Here it is on this map. West and east, it's between Quesnel and McBride; south and north, it's between Wells Gray and Bowron Lake provincial parks. And I'm told that it is vibrating with ferocious rainbow trout."

I was hooked.

"There's one catch," he continued. "We have two lots: the smaller one, a little over three acres, fronts on the shore, and we have full title. But title to the larger one behind, about twenty-one acres, is provisional on our building something on it."

"How do we get there?" I pressed on, inflamed with naive enthusiasm.

"The easy way is to charter a plane from Quesnel. But I think you ought to try approaching from the lake below. It would be more of an adventure, and it would give you a feel for the country. All you have to do is drive to the south shore of Quesnel Lake, paddle your canoe across and up the North Arm, and then hike up this valley (I think he said valley) to Mitchell Lake. There is supposed to be some kind of a trail." This was easy for Fred to say; however, organizing the other guys is his forte, and, as I said, I was hooked.

At the end of June 1975, we set off from Calgary bound for Cariboo country and Quesnel Lake. I was accompanied by my sixteen-year-old son, Rod, and his buddy Cam Dow in one pickup with a canoe on top, while Dave McIver and his two young sons, Kent and Brent, took another pickup and canoe. The plan was to make it up the "some kind of a trail" to the west end of Mitchell Lake with the canoes. But if we didn't arrive by a specific date, Fred would have us airlifted from the North Arm of Quesnel Lake. In either case, Fred would fly in with equipment and supplies to meet us at our property at the east end of Mitchell Lake and get us started on this sketchy homesteading escapade.

Turning off Highway 97 at 150 Mile House, we drove east to Horsefly and then north to Lowry's Lodge at Haggen's Point on the south shore of Quesnel Lake. There we met Howard Lowry, proprietor and guide, who assured us that there was a trail from the North Arm of Quesnel Lake up to Mitchell Lake.

On a clear morning and with our nerve revved up, we loaded both canoes and embarked on perfectly calm, blue-green water. A great beginning, especially when Rod insisted, "Dad, you sit in the middle and relax. Cam and I will paddle."

Trolling lines as we crossed the two- to three-mile stretch,

Dave and Cam each caught, in quick succession, dandy three-to-four-pound rainbows. Entering the North Arm, we pulled in to shore for a quick snack just beyond a point on the west side.

With a fourth cast from shore I connected. "Rod! Quick, bring the net!" I hollered. Like a locomotive, the trout surged out and jumped, surged and jumped again; the reel sang out. The rod butt was jammed in my belly and I was jabbering throughout. I alternately reeled, then let the trout run, gradually gaining on it. We got it in, and it was a beaut: a seven-pound rainbow trout brought in on a six-pound test line, a Len Thompson #7 spinner, in a fifteen-minute bout.

"Hey guys! How about this Quesnel Lake? Who needs Mitchell Lake?" I enthused.

After catching another couple of rainbow while proceeding up the arm, we realized that we were overstocked for supper. On spotting people at a cottage, we pulled in and met Mr. and Mrs. Stan Barrett. They were more than happy to take three fish. Fortunately for us, Stan knew the area, having trapped it years ago. "Yes," he affirmed, "there is a trail up to Mitchell. About three miles up the river, you'll come to two old, soddy cabins, and that's where the trail starts. Don't miss the cabins. Beyond that, the river is much too tough." This was the specific information we needed.

We reached the end of the North Arm and the mouth of the Mitchell River about midafternoon the following day. Faced with four channels, we had difficulty determining which was the main one and then holding to it, but with the McIvers following, onward and upward we paddled, Cam (stern) and Rod (bow) still wielding the paddles. "Dad, you just take it easy and enjoy the view—quietly," Rod ordered with a grin. I acceded to this quite willingly since I had to function as the mastermind of the expedition, and my brain works better when my body is immobile.

After a couple of miles of easy paddling, we pulled in to a suitable spot for a camp and enjoyed another trout supper. The

Starting from Lowry's Lodge on the south shore of Quesnel Lake; Kent and Brent in the first canoe and Rod, the author, and Cam in the second

Canoeing north across Quesnel Lake

Cam on the north arm of Quesnel Lake with a three-pound rainbow trout

Proceeding up Mitchell River

Brent, Kent, the author, Cam, and Rod at one of the two cabins three miles up Mitchell River

Kent and one of the many deadfalls on the trail to Mitchell Lake

Brent and Kent at the trail bridge

mosquitoes thought the spot suitable too, and I fought the buzzing insects most of the night.

Next day, with the splendid weather continuing, the ascent became gradually more strenuous as the current against us accelerated. We hove more closely to the right shore, which fortunately did prove to be the right side of the channel when we arrived at the old cabins with sod roofs at about 6 p.m.

I was uneasy about such a late start, but with Dave, Rod, and Cam eager to boot up the trail, I was outvoted. The idea was that we would sprint up with light packs to reconnoiter and camp, returning in the morning for a second haul. Unfortunately, with Rod and Cam bounding ahead and the youngest McIver spraining an ankle, we ended up strung out along the trail. I was in the middle, indecisive about either lagging back or spurting ahead, and no longer within earshot of either the rear or advance party.

It was getting dark when I came smack-dab up against an enormous deadfall. Unable to see where the trail continued on the other side of this huge, fallen tree, I was stumped. This was just another intimidating challenge of the B.C. rain forest. Groping around in all directions until it was completely dark, I actually managed to lose my landmark, the rotten old deadfall! Had Patrick McManus (an Idaho author of humorous outdoor stories) been with me, he could have written a whole book on the art of getting lost. Clueless and disgusted, I found a few square inches of open, uneven ground and crawled into my sleeping bag with the fervent hope that I could get back on track in the morning.

It finally got light enough to call it quits on trying to sleep. I lubricated my mouth with toothpaste and attempted to get my bearings. At least I could differentiate up-valley from down-valley, but the frustrating question was whether I was above or below the trail. Stumbling and lurching for a couple of hours, I angled downward and, with relief, soon intersected the path, which now looked to me like a transcontinental highway.

I trotted back down to the old cabins to rejoin both rear and advance parties. Rod and Cam had gone by me on their return hike but hadn't seen me. That's how far off the trail I had meandered, and that's rain forest for you. I gulped down half a quart of orange juice and resolved that when traveling alone the next time I would connect myself by string to the blocking windfalls.

My two bright boys reported that they had romped to the top and had even caught a couple of trout in Mitchell Lake for breakfast. The smart alecks remembered surmounting my arboreal Waterloo and figured that it was about a mile short of the top of a seven-mile trail. "Cheer up, old boy. At least we made it," they chortled.

It was obvious, especially to the "old boy," that we would not be able to haul a canoe up this overgrown, deadfall-punctuated trail. It was fortunate that we had plan B—the airlift—in reserve. Since it was July 4, and the floatplane was to arrive between July 8 and 10, we had four to six days to put in near the end of the North Arm of Quesnel Lake. Dave decided that his boys had had enough, so they embarked downstream for an early return to civilization.

Rod, Cam, and I set off in our canoe late that afternoon, enjoying a leisurely downstream run to the arm. En route, a loon played tag with us for a few minutes, and farther down we encountered five moose gulping an evening drink.

We eventually set up camp about a half mile south of the end of the arm at a pair of raft-cabins cabled to the shore; they appeared to be open to wayfarers. We would leave the premises clean and replenish the firewood supply in exchange for the small bit of sugar and tea that we used. Here we relaxed. I did a little reading, and the boys caught enough trout to augment our diminishing freeze-dried rations.

While on the deck one afternoon, I heard a rhythmic splashing and looked up from my book to see a scrawny, adolescent moose swimming past. I had no idea moose were such marathon swimmers. It seemed to be touring the arm, taking deep-water shortcuts across each cove.

On July 9, at 11 a.m., a Cessna floatplane arrived; the pilot, Gale Fowler, had spotted our orange raingear set out as markers. Gale had just deposited Fred at the east end of Mitchell Lake to wait for us. With fascination, I watched Gale meticuously lash the canoe to one pontoon.

"One time," he related, "I was doing this with a fellow's cherished birchbark canoe. I tightened the rope one final time and crunched the canoe to matchwood."

The flight up to Mitchell Lake gave us a splendid view of the upper silver-splinter stretch of the river as it roared down the canyon. In minutes we were at the top and cruising low over Mitchell Lake toward the east end. What a great first look I had at our new lake!

CHAPTER TWO

Endurance and Enjoyment

Mitchell Lake was below us. It was about ten miles long, between one and two miles wide, and circled by snow-spotted mountains whose uppermost peaks shouldered huge ice packs. Sunlit as it was on that day, Mitchell Lake appeared to be a darker blue-green than Quesnel Lake. As we approached the east end of Mitchell's vertical, wooded perimeter, something of a shoreline became visible.

So much natural beauty was difficult for me to absorb and appreciate at once. But that first, three-week stay at the lake sparked a remarkable development in my perception of nature, perception that would flourish over the next seventeen years.

Fred Brooks greeted us at the dock of the Executive Lodge, a neighboring retreat a cove away. Of course Fred could only spend a brief hour to help us get oriented. He had equipped us with a chain saw, nails, various tools, a tent, a 303 rifle, and a small mountain of food, which especially cheered up my crew. Fred pointed rather vaguely across the cove to indicate the general location of our property and then produced some kind of a map to further confuse me. "Go to it team!" he amiably shouted as he and the pilot took off on the trip back to the town of Quesnel. As I already knew, Fred has his own inimitable brand of unsophisticated delegation.

After selecting and clearing a spot on the east side of the cove where there was adequate shore space, we canoed our stuff across and erected two tents. After lunch we took a nap, the boys in the big tent and I in the pup tent with my head just inside the door. After a few minutes' rest, I heard heavy breathing just inches from my left ear. I turned my head and looked up into a large, black snout.

"Bear!" I yelped.

The snout retracted.

"What?" Rod responded from the next tent.

"Bear!" I repeated, somewhat agitated.

By the time the boys rallied to the call, our visitor had disappeared. We held a conference immediately, the main concern being our food supply.

"We've got to eliminate Mr. Bruin. It's him or us," my crew told me, practically in unison and not without exaggeration. I didn't argue.

We should have had the means to secure the food high up between trees, but in functioning as leader, I was typically underbriefed and underequipped. We had not planned for bears.

With our food supply vulnerably stacked on the ground under a flimsy polyethylene cover, the bear was sure to return, probably in about four hours. So at dusk we were waiting in the small tent to give the bear a clear approach to the food cache adjacent to the big tent.

"I hear him," whispered Cam, grabbing the rifle.

"That's him," seconded Rod, taking his bow and arrow in hand.

We peered out and clearly saw a bear (black, thankfully) poking its nose under the polyethylene. The mighty hunters moved to the attack. With teeth clamped to an edge of the cover, the bear rose on its hind legs. Cam fired. The bear fell back, writhed a few yards into the bush, and then dropped with a crash. The hunters advanced, Rod with his bow, rather rashly a bit ahead of Cam; I was very much in the rear. When they reached the bear, it was dead. One-shot Dow, we subsequently called Cam.

For hours into the night, Rod and Cam fervently skinned and butchered, trying to gain a few chunks of edible meat and a hide for a bear rug. Unfortunately, the carcass was infested with maggots or lice. I don't know which; I didn't want to look. The whole business depressed me. The boys ended up loading the whole lot into the canoe and dumping it in the middle of the lake.

To build a cabin, we first had to choose the site. It had to be on the back lot in order to qualify for completion of the title. My memory has dimmed a little on how we accomplished the seat-of-the-pants surveying, but I believe we eyeballed a straight line along one edge of the front lot, from the northwest survey pin (immediately discovered near the shore) to the northeast pin (found after a few hours of machete-hacking).

We were then able to extend the imaginary line east of the northeast pin (and therefore onto the back lot) to fix on a site a minimal distance from the shore and right next to a small stream. Having established this ideal spot for the cabin, we cleared a path back to the shore. The density of the trees and deadfalls steered us back to the northwest pin, on the other side of which stood an old plywood tent frame consisting of a floor and some half walls. We moved camp to this site and fitted our large tent over the existing structure. We hoped this setup would afford more secure food storage.

The next question of importance was the design of the cabin. Not being the least bit versed in the art of horizontal-and-corner-notched log construction, we decided to copy the simple vertical-log design of the Executive Lodge's utility cabin. We settled on a sixteen-foot by twelve-foot by six-foot gabled-roof structure with a four-foot wide deck—and began to build.

Selecting mostly spruce from the abundance of trees, we did

the felling pretty well within a hundred-yard radius. We cut logs of eighteen to twenty inches in diameter into sixteen-foot lengths and moved them with a come-along into position for floor joists. We built each wall like a picture frame: the sixteen-foot floor joist on the bottom, two six-foot vertical logs for the sides, and a sixteen-foot log across the top. Then we cut eight- to ten-inch diameter logs into six-foot lengths and fitted them into the picture frame.

The boys did the felling, cutting, and hauling; I did the fitting and nailing. A typical day was five to six hours' building; the remaining time was spent fishing and doing camp chores. Progress was doggedly sustained despite our having to work more and more in rain as the weather deteriorated. By the end of the second week, my plastic rainjacket was totally sap-encrusted, I should have hung onto it as a memento of pioneering perseverance.

Speaking of rain, one night it rained buckets. The gullies that formed in our loosely draped tent began to fill with rainwater that eventually dripped through onto us. The boys, of course, slept on with relatively little interruption, but I was miserably wet, cold, and unable to sleep. The best I could do was to get under my thoroughly soaked sleeping bag.

It was the longest night of my life and could have been the basis for an appropriate contribution to *A Fine and Pleasant Misery* by Patrick McManus. I questioned any power that might be as to why I was subjecting myself to this punishment. At that moment I fervently hated the place.

Wouldn't you know, the sun shone the next morning, and my enthusiasm was recharged. When they finally awoke, the crew members were their usual cheerful selves, just as if it had been a normal night. Oh, to sleep the sleep of the young!

While the boys typically slept soundly until 9 a.m., I was often unable to sleep past 5 a.m. regardless of the conditions, so the early morning was my fishing time. The fishing was good and challenging, especially the trolling while paddling. Stationary casting was less work but often not as productive.

My favorite stretch of water soon came to be "the shelf," which extends diagonally across the south corner of our end of the lake and is characterized by an abrupt drop in the level of the lake-bottom. Back and forth I would paddle and troll with the rod clamped between my legs. When a rainbow hit, I'd drop the paddle (in the canoe, most of the time), frantically grab the rod, and furiously reel in. This was not too smooth an operation, but great fun. I probably boated only one out of five of these scrappy rainbow, the "keepers" ranging from three-quarters to one-and-a-half pounds. I had to learn to reduce the tension on the reel, to let the rainbow run, and to keep the tip of the rod well up, especially during the jumps. The prospect of capture was better if I could hold the rainbow through three jumps.

One morning I quietly paddled into the mouth of what we were to call the Quiet River (actually the Christian River) at the south corner of the lake. There, in a relatively deep trench, I spotted several huge submarine-like fish. They had to be Dolly Varden. Nobody had told me about them being there. I hooked one on my reliable Len Thompson #8 spinner and for the first time experienced "dolly" action—the plunging, hard-pulling run-outs when you need to play the fish for a minimum of fifteen minutes.

I did get that first one in. With orange spots and a bull-like mouth, that Dolly Varden must have been close to six pounds. I hustled back to camp and tried to rouse Rod to take a picture.

"Aw Dad, I'm not awake yet. It's only eight o'clock. You'll catch another one."

Entirely irrational, I ordered, "Get up and take my picture."

In spite of my outburst, I did think the boys were performing valiantly, and we were getting along fine. I heartily recommend an outdoor expedition to improve father-son rapport. And Cam, adept and quietly affable, was a natural outdoorsman. Whether this was by nature or nurture, I don't know. But anybody who can cook reasonably good pancakes on an open fire in the rain has my enduring admiration. His droll version of the movie *Jeremiah Johnson*, which he claimed to have seen six times, was the entertainment feature at a couple of evening campfires.

One day, our neighbors from the lodge in the next cove paid us a visit at the work site. This delegation was led by Jim Harkey, the principal owner of the Executive Lodge. At the moment of their appearance, I had in my hand their double-edged axe, which I had the need and the nerve to borrow when no one was there.

"Isn't that my axe?" Mr. Harkey inquired, his visage tight-lipped.

"Why, yes," I managed to mumble. "I . . . I hope you don't mind. We . . . we broke ours. I'll be sure to return it." Embarrassed to the hilt, I could only hope that he could view this as an opportunity to be neighborly in the old, pioneering sense. He, however, simply switched topics.

"Just what are you doing?"

"We're building a cabin on our property," I replied, somewhat defensively.

"If you think this is your property, you're operating from scanty information," chipped in one of his aides.

"We've applied for the title to this lot. You're building this thing for us," Mr. Harkey concluded.

All I could mutter as they departed was that I thought we had the ownership papers. Assertive I could not be, however, since my understanding of the details of Fred's acquisition was incomplete. Subsequently, Fred did furnish me with the complete legal papers, and I have since gotten to know Mr. Harkey quite well and to appreciate his wry sense of humor. Someday I'll ask him what he was up to on that occasion.

Into the third week, and with improved weather, we labored. Gale Fowler had flown in plywood for the roof and the floor. Rod and Cam worked so well under my occasionally unsure direction that I had decided to give them the lead in building the gables and roof. I soon became apprehensive, however, about the pitch of the roof. Was it steep enough?

Cutting and splitting cedar shingles (shakes) was a learning experience. We got the roof tar-papered but only three-quarters shaked because we had to abandon work after breaking yet a second hatchet head, our improvised splitter.

Hard at it on the second-to-last day before our departure, we were visited again by Executive Lodge neighbors. They were two of Jim Norman's married daughters, who had flown in for a family vacation at the lodge after the Harkey group flew out. Rod and Cam took great delight in giving them the tour, and the women were impressed.

"You've worked hard, and it must have been difficult," one of them remarked.

The boys beamed.

Looking at our primitive cabin, the other added, "And to think that we've been complaining that our dishwasher didn't work."

On our last night, we slept in the almost-completed cabin. What a treat to be under a rainproof roof (even though the weather was now clear) and to enjoy the relative comfort of a wooden structure!

Wednesday, July 26, was our last day. Gale was due about 3 p.m. We were packed and ready with all our gear on the shore. We waited. And waited. About 4:30 p.m., we heard a plane—not Gale's. Waiting patiently for the plane would always be a challenge for me.

After another last look at our achievement, we returned to the shore to wait some more and discovered that bears had made off with two packages of trout, one fresh and one smoked.

Gale arrived shortly after 6 p.m., and we had a pleasant flight back to Lowry's Lodge on Quesnel Lake. The fishing-derby smorgasboard was going full tilt, and we were invited to fill our tummies.

On the drive back to Calgary, the boys both expressed their willingness to return the next summer. This really impressed me. I was thoroughly pooped, and my feelings were mixed. But memories of the bad times (being lost in the forest, trying to sleep soaking wet, working with wet logs, cooking in the rain) would be overruled by the upbeat memories (a rainbow strike or a dolly plunge, a clear daybreak out on the lake, a reflection of moonlight on rippling water) and by the camaraderie. We had established our own place, a retreat to do our own thing at our own pace for years to come.

CHAPTER THREE

The Summers Come and Go

There was never any doubt about continuing the Mitchell project, but I couldn't seem to muster the energy to go in the second summer. I settled for a leisurely canoeing-camping circuit of Quesnel Lake with friend Del Sharpe. Fred Brooks, however, managed to mobilize my son Rod and three of Rod's buddies. They flew in with a boat and motor and built bunks and tables in the cabin.

A government official inspected the cabin, found the roof inadequate, and put a hold on the title completion. So the third summer, 1977, Fred Brooks and I went in for ten days in August to rebuild the roof.

From Lowry's Lodge on Quesnel Lake, we motored easily to the mouth of the Mitchell River. There were so many sweepers—trees and branches stuck in the riverbed—creating a hazard to navigation that every fifteen to twenty minutes our passage was blocked. Fred would hang on to a sweeper while I "swede-sawed" branches or trunks so that we could scrunch through. It eventually struck me that the current was faster and the river narrower than they should be.

"Fred, we've passed the old cabins. We've overshot them. How did I miss seeing them?" I wailed.

"We've been pretty busy with sweepers, and it's getting a bit dark," Fred rationalized. "If we missed them on the way up, we can't count on seeing them going back down. We better pull in to this cove, and I'll look for the trail. You stay put and relax."

This order sounded familiar.

Stay put I did, cussing my blindness and a few thousand mosquitoes. Fred barged uphill through the forest. An hour and a half later, and with little light left, he returned. He had found the trail. What a relief! Since it was quite obvious that this was no place to camp for the night, we decided to foot it up the trail in the dark, exactly against my resolution made that first summer after the encounter with the giant deadfall. Why was I making a habit of nighttime hiking?

We secured the boat, shouldered packs, and, with one flashlight and some moonlight, struggled through forest for forty-five minutes until we intersected the old trail. Fred had performed as the qualified and licensed guide that he was. I was mightily impressed.

The going was easier now, but Fred was stopped by a charley horse. Not surprising, considering the effort he'd made. He swallowed a painkiller, I took on the heavier pack, and late that night we arrived at the top.

Lowry's canoe, motor, and paddles were stashed where they were supposed to be, and we were still hyped enough that we agreed to carry on. Anyway, the terrain was bad for camping. The motor refused to fire though, so we had to paddle. We also had to bail because the canoe leaked. We sang a few snatches of some song or other to keep up our spirits. After more than an hour, we spotted something of a sandy shoreline. Exhausted, we pulled in and before sacking out made do with a handful of granola. We hadn't had a meal since 8 a.m., a good way to lose weight in jig time.

Next morning, we discovered that we were just a few yards short of the Northern Lights Lodge, which was about a quarter of

The first cabin

Don, Gil, and Rod

Gil with a rainbow trout

the way to our end of the lake. An employee of the lodge towed us to our place. Bless kind, congenial Barbara from Colorado.

The rebuilding of the roof was stymied by a chain saw that would not start: it had been sitting under a drip for a year and was all gummed up. Fred, basically a mechanical engineer, spent all of the first day reviving it. Throughout the next five days, and mainly in rain, we tore off the roof, cut and mounted new rafters and gables, and cut and split shakes—all to construct a higher-pitched roof. The roof later passed inspection, enabling us to gain full title to our Mitchell retreat.

Demonstrating the ultimate in frontier neighborliness, Barbara came for us on the sixth day to tow us back to the west end. We galloped down the trail to the turnoff, which Fred had methodically marked, and made our way easily—and in daylight for a change—to the little cove on the river and to our motorboat.

In preparing to embark for the run down the river, we were flabbergasted to see a stream-wide procession of fish slowly swimming upstream.

"Are they trout? Are they rainbow or dolly? They're all about the same size, three or four pounds, and reddish-colored," I observed, dumbfounded.

"Let's see if we can catch one. You try your Len Thompson," Fred suggested.

My efforts did not distract them one whit. Then the penny finally dropped: they were salmon—spawning salmon. We later figured that they must have made their ritualistic, laborious way up the Fraser River to the Quesnel River, into Quesnel Lake and up the North Arm, then up Mitchell River. But how much farther up? I promised myself I would retrace the trip another year to find out where the salmon go to spawn, for upriver the flow soon increases to semi-waterfall velocity.

Drifting downstream and carefully poling past the sweepers, we soon came abreast of the elusive twin soddy cabins. We had overshot them by about a mile on the way up. About three miles down this approximately four-mile stretch of river, we appeared to have passed all the timber obstacles, so Fred started the motor. We motored slowly and carefully and then, just as we had started to breathe more easily, the propeller hit a submerged rock and one blade was knocked off.

Up to this point, Fred had displayed a great deal of patience, fortitude, and good nature, but this was beyond even his limit. I recall that he exclaimed something a little stronger than his usual "Oh, fuzz!" So it was half speed on the lower lake to Lowry's, which we finally reached about 2 a.m.

Early the next morning, Fred deposited me at the bus station in Williams Lake on his way up to Vanderhoof. When I boarded the bus, I was grizzly-bearded, several days unbathed, wearing the same dirty duds in which I had arrived. At 100 Mile House, a young fellow took the seat next to me and opened conversation.

"Have you been prospecting or trapping?" he queried, eyeing my primitive appearance.

"Neither. I've been working on a cabin at an upper lake," I sleepily replied.

"Oh. What do you do for a living?" he pressed on.

"I'm a high school teacher in Calgary," I answered mechanically.

Either this disclosure disappointed him or he thought I was bonkers because he mumbled some excuse and moved to another seat.

The next summer, 1978, I had a vastly different experience at Mitchell Lake. My friend Art Yates came with me, and we started with a leisurely flight from Quesnel with Gale Fowler. This was to be a holiday for a change: two weeks of relaxing, fishing, and simply enjoying the place. And the weather was perfect. Nevertheless, I was troubled by spasms of ambivalence. How were we going to fill in all the time?

The first hours and days seemed so long. Since I had no major project to tackle, I had to learn to gear down to a slower pace. Art showed me how to do this.

We had flown in a dandy wood-burning cookstove that Fred had somehow acquired. So we did have the job on the first day of lugging the stove from the shore to the cabin and installing it. What a treat to cook on it after having made do with a "puffing billy" heating stove.

Art was relaxed and consistently in good spirits. I especially enjoyed his whistling and singing march tunes. (We had both been members of the Edmonton Schoolboys Band back in the late thirties, although we hadn't known each other then.) At the lake, Art taught me how to listen: how to distinguish, for example, the call of the crow from the call of the raven. And he was an excellent cook.

Furthermore, Art set an example in good sportsmanship. When he lost a rainbow, he doffed his cap and said, "Here's to you, my finny friend. You won that battle fair and square." I was still inclined to cry a bit. He had compassion for the trout too. He good-naturedly insisted on killing the "keepers," once boated, more promptly than I had ever bothered to do. And when we started to catch too many, he filed the barbs off the triple-hooks on one of his spinners so that he could release the "non-keepers" much more easily.

And the fishing! One day at the mouth of the Christian River, I hooked a five-pound dolly on my stock #8 Len Thompson just when I was thinking I should be using a #7 because of all the submerged logs and branches at that spot. This trout immediately pulled down and headed toward the logs. I reeled, but the trout kept pulling out.

"It won't come—I can't gain on it. It's going to snag on the lumber," I moaned.

"Take your time and keep your tip up. I'll back-paddle the

boat out slowly," Art directed.

The dolly had begun to tire but still had enough energy to swim away from Art's submerged net each time I moved the fish toward it. My right hand became quite numb. Finally, we had the dolly netted and boated.

Another fine day gave us some excitement while trolling. Art had just connected with a rainbow when a bald eagle wheeled overhead and, with talons hooked, swooped low at the rainbow, which was at the height of its first jump. The eagle missed, thank goodness! Imagine a rainbow and an eagle linked on a six-pound line! As the eagle flew off, we admired its white head, yellow beak, and five-foot wingspan.

Another time, we sighted two moose grazing in the reeds at the south corner of our end of the lake. They appeared to be a cow and a calf. The darker and larger one quickly disappeared into the woods as we motored closer; the smaller one dallied a few seconds to gawk at us before following.

One morning, when we were just up, we looked out of the window and saw that a huge tree, probably three feet in diameter, had uprooted (the way they do in the soft earth of the rain forest) during the night. It had fallen across the trail only thirty feet from the cabin. And we hadn't heard a thing.

The following summer I brought a new companion to Mitchell Lake, Gil Menzies, assistant principal of the high school in Calgary where I taught. We had hit it off well right from the start, especially after I introduced the subject of Mitchell Lake. Gil said flat out: "I want to go in with you." Here was a kindred spirit, I thought, unaware that this was only a half truth. He was in fact more of a fishing maniac than I was.

The upshot was that in July of 1979, Gale Fowler flew Gil and me, each with a son, in to Mitchell. It was the last flight with Gale; soon after, he sold out to Gideon Schuetze of Williams Lake and returned to the United States.

My son Rod, now twenty-one, had just returned from an exhausting two-year church mission in Austria. Our trip was to be a recuperative holiday for him. He didn't spend every hour fishing as we did, but he was in his own space part of the time and enjoyed simply loafing around the homestead. And for once I was intelligent enough to leave him be. After all, he'd proved himself here in that first strenuous summer.

Gil's fifteen-year-old son, Don, was keen on the fishing, and when it slowed down, he proved to be as innovative as his dad at switching from spinners to bait. But he, too, had a limit for putting up with his old man.

One day, I got Gil fired up to try a hike up to Christian Lake. Howard Lowry (of Lowry's Lodge on Quesnel Lake) had mentioned that the rainbow at Christian Lake fought so hard that they would straighten out the hook on a spinner, and our neighbors at the Executive Lodge confirmed that there was a negotiable trail. We persuaded Rod and Don to come along.

We found the start of the trail near the remains of a cabin west of Hooker's Point. The four of us plodded forward at a good pace for about a mile, with the trail easily discernible because of the saw cuts in the deadfall. At one point, we came across an ancient trap chain still fixed in the hollow of a tree. Gaining some altitude, we came out of the forest and crossed the shale base of the first mountain on the west side of the valley. We were then into dense, second-growth jungle. There was no trace of a trail. We had to push aside thick brush, including devil's club, at every other step. Progress was slow. Our hands were working harder than our feet. We had to guess that we were still aiming south and up valley because visibility was nil.

We broke through to a clearing where the high grass had been matted down very recently because it seemed to be steaming. Gil and I simultaneously thought—but were almost afraid to say—

"Oh-oh, probably a bear's nest and quite possibly grizzly." Momentarily cowed, but soon regaining our drive, we struggled on. Gil and I were getting more foul-tempered by the minute. It had become a battle to the end: us against the jungle.

The two sons in the rear were thoroughly fed up by this time, Don especially. He was critical of the whole operation. "Dad, don't you ever know when to quit? We're not getting anywhere—let's go back!"

"What's the matter with you?" Gil cranked back. "I've come this far; I'm not going to quit."

"Lighten up, Dad!" Don persisted. "Let's head back and go fishing."

After a few more minutes of clawing our way, we were utterly blocked. Gil and I came to our senses and admitted defeat. The negotiable trail was a myth.

CHAPTER FOUR

Paddle, Hike, and Paddle

The idea of getting into Mitchell Lake via the lower lake and trail, as we had done twice before, still intrigued me. Flying was certainly a breeze, but it was an expense others were not always keen to share. Furthermore, the Quesnel Lake—-Mitchell River route was an adventure in itself. The tough part, logistically, was getting from the west to the east end of Mitchell Lake.

In August 1980, Pat O'Brien, Ron Lewis, Rick Lewis, and I drove from Calgary to Horsefly in two vehicles. Pat drove his "Jimmy" with his Grummond canoe on top, and I drove my Toyota pickup with my Frontiersman canoe on top. After we had set up camp that evening on the outskirts of Horsefly, I phoned George, manager of the Northern Lights Lodge on Mitchell Lake, who was headquartered at Likely. When I had phoned him in July, he assured me, I thought, that somebody would be at the Northern Lights Lodge in August to help us get to our end of the lake. I came out of the phone booth totally deflated. "He says . . . that there's nobody at the lodge," I stammered. "The bookings were cancelled."

The other three laughed at my stricken state. "Cheer up, old Bill! We'll make it somehow," Pat declared. Their optimistic response revived me. With this kind of spirit and camaraderie, what could stop us?

But another jab of fate lay in wait. Waking early the next morning, I saw the sun's first rays penetrating through a slit in the bottom of my overturned canoe.

On reaching Lowry's Lodge on Quesnel Lake, I was able to borrow a patching kit to repair the slit. Pat then satisfied himself that the gear in both canoes was securely lashed, and we embarked. Rick got into the bow of my canoe with a strained smile, though he seemed confident enough. Perhaps this wasn't the best introduction to canoeing. The canoe did leak, but minimally; we were stroking well and keeping up with the other canoe.

I hollered ahead, "Hey, how about stopping at this point and trying some fishing?" I was thinking of the seven-pound rainbow I had caught there the first year.

"Let's travel now while the water is calm. We'll fish later," Pat, the sensible one, replied.

I conceded. That evening we caught a few rainbow for supper after making camp on the west shore of the North Arm.

On the second day, we paddled up the North Arm and made a second onshore camp. The site was left immaculate the next morning, with Pat insisting that we take out the garbage we hadn't burned. By early afternoon we reached the end of the arm, and with "Captain" Pat O'Brien's craft leading, we paddled uneventfully up Mitchell River. The sweepers seemed minimal compared to those encountered on the motorboat ascent Fred and I had made.

Daylight was still with us when I spotted the two soddy cabins on the other side of the river; the tricky part would be crossing from the west side to the east side, for the current was racing. Pat and Ron deftly crossed over first. Then Pat hollered instructions to apply a stroke that was new to me, a pry stroke, I think it was. I concentrated intently, and we surged across successfully. Never having taken a course in canoeing, I was fully willing to accept leadership in such a crucial situation.

So, there we were at the soddy cabins and the foot of the trail to Mitchell Lake. After a quick, cold supper, we secured the canoes in a willow clump and loaded our backpacks. I was amazed at the size and weight of Pat's pack.

"What have you got in there, Pat?" I inquired.

"It's mainly my friend's tent, and there's no way I'm going to leave it here," he resolutely replied.

I couldn't josh him out of it, but I chortled to myself that he wasn't as smart about hiking and packs as he was about canoeing.

It was 5 p.m., a couple of hours earlier than it had been at this point back on our first journey in 1975. It took me a mere fifteen minutes to rediscover the start of the trail to Mitchell Lake before we were off and plodding. Rick and Ron started off in good spirits but later tired a bit. A grim-visaged Ron thumped silently into one of the rest stops but regained his customary good nature before we pushed on. All three razzed me about my seven-mile estimate, swearing that only a crow could make it valid. The most strenuous task for me was helping Pat put on his gargantuan pack after each rest stop. I was pleased that we were able to follow the trail with only momentary hesitation at a few obscure spots.

We made the top and the west end of Mitchell Lake just as daylight was fading. With heart in mouth, I inspected the Lowrys' stationed canoe. Mrs. Lowry had said that she thought, but wasn't sure, that it had been replaced or repaired. I was instantly disappointed.

"Rotten luck, guys," I muttered. "This is the same old leaky canoe."

"Let's try it. Maybe it'll get us to Northern Lights," replied our indomitable Irishman.

"Even if we drown to death?" I asked in an attempt to be jocular. However, I was lighthearted enough because it seemed that we just could not be stopped.

In faint moonlight, Pat and I shoved off in the leaky canoe, just as Fred and I had done three years earlier. The Lewis brothers were happy to stay put for the night, with the assurance that I would motor back for them the following day.

The leaking was worse than before, and bailing was almost futile. Every ten minutes or so, we had to pull in to shore, stumble around on the rocks in the water, overturn the canoe and dump the water out. We eventually made it to the Northern Lights Lodge, found it unoccupied, as expected, and spotted four aluminum boats. As we sacked out for the night on the beach, I could hear the sandflies buzzing, "Goody gumdrops—Old Bill's back."

Starting at dawn the next day made it possible to paddle the remaining seven miles to the east end of the lake before the water got too rough from the typical late-morning wind. The boat we elected to borrow had oarlocks, but there were no oars in sight.

"How are we going to propel it, Pat?" I laughingly inquired, thinking, You're stumped now.

"We'll paddle!" confidently replied my man. We did have the paddles from the leaky canoe.

Why had I thought Pat would be deterred at this stage? So we paddled, with Pat in the stern and me in the bow. Every few minutes he piped, "Change!" and we slid across to dig in at the opposite side.

It was a long seven miles, but Mitchell Lake remained virtually unrippled. After three hours of paddling, we arrived at the homestead. What a glorious sight! Our trip was an achievement that we would later recollect with zest.

Leaving Pat to look the place over, I motored back to the west end to collect Ron and Rick. Quite relieved to see me, they reported that they had spent a comfortable enough night bedded on a ledge and had enjoyed a trout breakfast. This reminded me that I hadn't eaten anything except mountain mix for what seemed like several hundred hours. When we got back to the homestead, Pat told us about an encounter with one of our resident bears.

Our week at the homestead was simply grand, and worth the suspense, stress, and sweat. The weather was near perfect, and the fishing lived up to my billing. Fishing four-in-a-boat was a bit of a test, with Pat requiring more space for his big precast windup. We had to be tolerant because he was the camp cook, and a superb one even though he insisted on poaching the dollies. We didn't all stick to boat fishing, anyway. Ron, for one, discovered the fun of bobber fishing at the stream we called Americans Creek.

On the third day, we returned the borrowed aluminum boat to the Northern Lights Lodge and wondered how we could store our own boat at the west end of the lake for the winter. Our solution was to build a miniature house, complete with a shake roof, to store the boat's motor and to stash the boat alongside it. This storage shed was completed in combination with a fun day of fishing at the west end.

Making an early start on departure day, we motored to the west end of the lake, stashed the motor and boat, and romped down the trail with considerably lighter packs—except for Pat's. About three-quarters of the way down the trail, we came upon a group of about twenty kids with three mothers and one barrel-torsoed man.

And how about this? They were hauling huge packs of food and two canoes, ascending the trail in a shuttle procedure. They appeared to be taking the packs up a stretch then leaving them to repeat the "lift" with a second set of packs. Two of the bigger boys together carried a canoe on their shoulders, with a smaller one leading to call the turns and clear the way. The man was carrying the second canoe by himself.

He was the Reverend Ernie Gonzalles, a veritable twentieth-century coureur de bois, from Pine Valley, B.C. He told us that this was an annual expedition by boat from Likely, at the west end of Quesnel Lake, then up the Mitchell River to the soddy cabins. From there, they make the Herculean ascent to Mitchell Lake and set up camp somewhere on the south shore, a short distance from the west end.

It was an awesome and deflating encounter! We had been feeling proud of our shank's-mare achievement with—it hurts to add—a single pack on each back.

Coasting down Mitchell River from the soddy cabins was uneventful: that is, we didn't hit anything. On arriving at the North Arm, we pulled up onto a sandbar at the river's mouth to reorganize our gear. It was midafternoon. Clear and calm. A calm, at that moment, functioning as a vacuum. For heading up the arm directly toward us with alarming speed was a black twister. It was momentarily mesmerizing.

Scrambling frantically, my three companions got into their rainsuits, pulled up the canoes and overturned them just as the squall hit. (I'd left my rainsuit back at the cabin—wouldn't need it!) While the others held the canoes down, I found some degree of shelter in a huge, partly hollowed log. The storm was over in less than forty minutes, and then the sun shone again. What luck that we hadn't embarked minutes earlier!

It had been a rouser of a trip!

CHAPTER FIVE

Four Men
in a Boat

By the summer of 1981, Gil Menzies was hooked on Mitchell Lake. He was keen to return every summer but made it clear that he was through with hikes to Christian Lake, or anyplace else—period. Being the natural enthusiast that he is, he wanted to share our exclusive retreat with friends. In the early eighties, he recruited others, a pair at a time, to fly in with us for a week or more. After all, we had four bunks and a roomy fiberglass boat, and Gil enjoyed cooking—so why not make it a foursome?

Although our setup was primitive, the cabin was rainproof and holding up fine—except for the door. We discovered on one arrival that bears had easily gnashed or slashed through the flimsy, cardboard-filled door and messed up the cabin's interior. We guessed that they had been rampaging for eats upon emerging from hibernation in the spring. We patched and remounted the door, but the bears repeated their break-and-enter. We finally built a secure door with double plywood and a tin liner.

In the way of utilities for the cabin, we had a Coleman lantern and the stream a few feet from the door for running water. Our cookstove, operated mainly by Gil, produced great pancake brunches and fish suppers. Gil recalls that some of us ate as many as nine trout each at a sitting, but he must be exaggerating. Dishes were washed outside, usually by me, on a plywood table where one could slop both the wash and rinse water with wild abandon.

A two-minute walk away, the biffy was a bench with a store-bought seat, which had to be replaced when a rare trespasser swiped it. The lake was our bathtub. July days were usually warm enough to tough it out with a soap-up and a plunge plus a few strokes in the lake if the water temperature was reasonable. A wash basin and a small mirror affixed to a tree served for personal washing and grooming. Coping with contact lenses (I'm the only one who has had to) was troublesome but manageable. I remember one guest good-humoredly regretting that he had to do without his hairdryer.

We were comfortable enough in the cabin, although that's easy for me to say since I had dibs on a lower bunk. I did give up my luxurious lower bunk one time to watch the nightly rodent rodeo. The mice seemed to thrive on mouse-seed poison, and our conventional, cheese-baited trap scored infrequently. There must have been a mouse waiting-to-join membership list a mile longer than the one for humans at the Glencoe Club in Calgary.

I once tried setting a better mousetrap. Designed by Carolyn Brooks, it was a wheel over water that the mouse had to surmount to get to the cheese bait. Well, I stayed awake half one night listening to one of these romping rodents spin the wheel continuously. Finally, I heard a splash and thought, We got ya at last—now drown! Next morning, there was no drowned mouse and not a trace of the cheese. Why didn't these wily little acrobats keep anyone else awake?

There were plenty of insects: no-see-ums, mosquitoes, deerflies, horseflies. Ravaged the first day or two, our skin would get some relief only when there was no virgin territory left. The insects especially seemed to know when both hands were busy, as when we were pouring gas.

When recruiting guests, Gil tended to oversell the accommodations a bit. He did not, however, oversell the fishing: it consistently equaled or exceeded expectation. We were usually on the verge of being overstocked since we did not have any refrigeration.

There was shoreline fishing and paddle-your-own-canoe fishing, but serious fishing expeditions meant that four of us would board the fiberglass boat powered by a four-horsepower Johnson motor and head west to fish several lively creek mouths. Typically, Gil would be in the stern to drive the boat and determine destinations and durations; the two guests had to be content to share the middle seat, and I would be on the bow seat. While we were stationary off a creek mouth, I would sit facing forward on the prow with my feet dangling just above the water; this gave me plenty of space and water in front for casting. It also, of course, opened up more casting room for the other three. Not entirely selfish, I periodically offered this choice spot to the others but never had a taker—maybe they were afraid of falling in.

The casting generally proceeded in a gentlemanly manner with few clashes or entanglements. Ironically, the only mishap occurred when just the two of us, Gil and I, were fishing from the boat. To this day I'm not sure how he did it: he put a spinner hook through one of my ear lobes.

"Gil, you're going to have to do something about this," I reacted, exercising some control, "and I mean NOW!"

"Hold still. Don't say another word," he responded.

Well, he had his knife at my ear, the point inserted alongside the hook and barb, and the extraction completed before I could realize it. And I hardly felt a thing. I razzed him about his sloppy casting but also had to commend him for his split-second surgery.

Gil's guests seemed to enjoy a sojourn of seven to ten days at Mitchell Lake, although only one of them returned a second time. For some of them, it was probably just a half notch up from a camping trip you're keener to get home from than you were to launch. But there were no complaints, each guest sustaining a sporting spirit—what we later realized was a spirit of endurance for two or three of them. It was a grin-and-bear-it attitude that had sustained those few.

One guest, Bob Haslam, caught our best fish ever, a ten-pound dolly, at the west end. Bob finally got the monster reeled in; I was in the water and had just managed to net it.

"Lift it up," Gil hollered.

"I can't—it's too heavy; I've got to plant my feet better," I responded.

The three of us managed to complete the capture, but Bob didn't say much while Gil and I enthused for the next few hours. It occurs to me now that Bob is individualistic enough that he can't be button-pushed to join the raving of others. On the drive back to Calgary from Williams Lake, although it was a particularly hot day, Bob adamantly vetoed stopping for a swim in a dirty-looking lake. He was back in his own saddle. I thought Bob the least likely of our guests to return to Mitchell Lake, yet he is the only one who did.

CHAPTER SIX

An Alternative Route

"Let's see if we can find another route into Mitchell Lake," Fred said to me one day in the spring of 1983. "According to this map we should be able to drive to the base of the Mitchell River valley."

"Yes," I replied, "the lumber industry has extended harvesting in that area. Flying out last summer, I saw a new clearing on the north side about a third of the way up the valley."

"We could cut a trail up the valley from that clearing," Fred continued optimistically.

It was clear by this time that if Fred was going to make any use of our Mitchell property, we would have to establish ground access. His sense of proprietorship would not be complete until he could drive to the place, or at least to a point within hiking distance. Since he was the partner, I was willing to explore the possibility of a reasonable ground route to the homestead. I had begun to realize, however, that the essential value of our Mitchell was its inaccessibility.

In early June, I set out with Fred and my middle son, Ken, in Fred's truck with provisions, maps, binoculars, surveyor's ribbon, and machetes. We turned off Highway 97 at McLeese Lake, drove to Likely, and then went north to the Cariboo–Maeford forestry road turnoff, just short of Keithley Creek. Proceeding on this gravel road to Maeford Lake, we stopped to camp for the night opposite a muddy road into private property. Walking down the gravel road, we met Cliff Wilson and his dad. They were the licensed guides and outfitters for the area north of Mitchell River. Expressing interest in our expedition, they confirmed the remainder of the route to the advanced lumber clearing on the north side of the Mitchell River valley. They also encouraged us to look for something of a trail up the north side of the valley to Mitchell Lake, but this was pretty vague, and I was becoming skeptical of trail reports.

Next morning, we drove past a deserted lumber camp to a fork in the road approximately ninety miles from McLeese Lake. We followed the east branch of the fork to a new bridge over Cameron Creek. This road apparently led up to the advanced clearing. Curious about the other road, we turned around at the bridge, drove back to the fork and down the south branch until it became too rutted and intersected with washouts to travel. Then we got out and walked to where we could see the end of the North Arm of Quesnel Lake.

Returning by truck to the Cameron Creek bridge, we followed the east branch road all the way to the advanced clearing, then walked the length of this plateau from west to northeast as it curved around the mountainside. From the easternmost point, we could see up the valley leading to Mitchell Lake.

Fred decided we would pursue a route along the northern ridge of this valley, even though a deep, deadfall-filled ravine barred our way immediately ahead. We plunged downward to avoid the impassable ravine and hoped that we would find a way back up later in the route.

After tightening our boots and packs, we lurched, stumbled, and groped through rain forest at its thickest. Soon after reaching river level, we found and followed an eastward saw-cut trail; it disappeared after fifteen yards or so, leaving us to battle thick forest again. We came onto game trails that soon petered out. It seemed hopeless. We slogged our way southward through and around bogs to the river's edge, where we recovered our sense of direction.

Fred took a compass-and-map reading to determine the best way back to the Cameron Creek bridge and the truck. It was 5 p.m., and I had never been more pooped.

"I say, Fred, are we going to be stuck in this jungle for the night?" I inquired.

"No fear! We'll make it back to the truck before dark," replied our intrepid guide. And we did—just.

At breakfast the next morning Ken, Fred, and I had to concede partial defeat. The one option, we agreed, was to return to the viewpoint on the south-branch road, strike a route to a point above the confluence of Cameron Creek and Mitchell River, somehow cross these waterways to the south side of the valley, and then implement a trail to intersect the existing trail I had become so fond of along the southern ridge, the trail that led to Mitchell Lake from the soddy cabins.

Flagging the first stretch (about a mile and a half) to the confluence was relatively easy. We avoided some of the dense undergrowth by following ridges, game trails, and a short, previously flagged path. At the confluence, we found that we could wade across Cameron Creek but not across Mitchell River.

A scheme to cross the river would have to wait because Fred couldn't give this expedition any more time. At least we could be pleased about two accomplishments: eliminating the notion of a route along the northern ridge of the valley and initiating access to the existing southern ridge trail from the south-branch road on the northern ridge.

Ken and I returned in mid-July via the Maeford route with the objective of reaching Mitchell Lake. Ken's directional sense and landmark-fixing skills were superior to mine, and his geophysical field experience and enthusiasm for the outdoors made him a good partner. We left the truck at the south-branch road and hiked the approximate mile and a half along our flagged path to the confluence of Cameron Creek and Mitchell River. Mitchell River was higher and wider than it had been in June. Could we cross it? First we would have to improvise a bridge. That was the challenge.

Searching for a tree that was close to the bank and high enough that its length would traverse the width of the river, we selected a pine about three and a half feet in diameter at the base. It leaned slightly toward the river and was, we hoped, sufficiently tall. I marked it, and we returned to the truck to set up camp.

It was overcast the next morning when we started clearing our flagged route with machete, axe, and chain saw. Ken and I hacked for an hour, cutting only a quarter of the way along. We decided that since the remainder of the trail was passable, we would switch to the crucial challenge—the river crossing.

So, there we were confronting the marked tree by the river with the Husqvarna in hand. I had never tackled a tree this large, so I checked the instruction booklet. I was tense and determined to get the cut right. About four feet up, we scored the front wedge and, taking turns, made bottom and top cuts that intersected almost two-thirds through. After knocking the front wedge out, we turned the saw off and took a breather.

We had resumed and cut three inches into the back when the saw quit. After repeated efforts to start it and keep it going for more than a few seconds, we had to admit that we were beaten, if only temporarily. Surely we could get it going by the next morning after it had cooled off—dried out—or whatever? There was a lesson in this: carry a freshly shop-tuned saw or, better still, two freshly shop-tuned saws.

Continuing the expedition was entirely dependent on completing the felling of the tree. Being unqualified in chain saw mechanics, I decided that the best bet was to drive back that evening to ask the Wilsons on Maeford Lake Road for help. They had certainly been interested in our project.

It was showering on and off along the seven-mile stretch to the Wilsons' place. Cliff and his dad were at home and were able to revive the Husqvarna for us.

On the return to camp, it was raining harder than before. As we got onto the last two miles of ungravelled road, we got stuck. Ever tried to put on chains in the dark, in the mud? We were thankful that three lumber-company guys came along and gave us a deft demonstration in chain installation. Wet, muddy, cold, famished, and exhausted, Ken and I finally made it back to camp. Never mind! Tomorrow, we would forge ahead.

The next morning was overcast but not raining. Ken hacked out more trail with the axe as I strode ahead with the saw. Arriving at the tree, I couldn't wait to get at the back cut. The saw started pronto, and I easily extended the back cut the necessary several inches.

"Hurry, Ken! It's going down." I hollered as the mighty pine protested, creaked at the cut, hesitated, then plunged down and across the river with a reverberating thud.

"I heard," Ken said with a grin as he arrived at the scene.

The tree was down, and we had a bridge. "Darn! It didn't go all the way across. We're a few feet short," I noted in looking again.

"It's all right," Ken countered. "The tip is down on a sandbar. It'll be easy wading the rest of the way."

The end of the butt, more than three feet in diameter, had not slipped off the stump; our lower front cut had not angled upward enough. We would never be able to budge it! No problem. With its tip buried in sand, the bridge was firmly fixed, and the ample width of the trunk, the sure-tread bark, and the upturned branches for handholds contributed to a safe, easy crossing over the raging river. We were soon on the south bank.

We waited out a rainshower and, after a quick snack, pressed on, continuing to find and flag a trail up the slope toward the trail by the soddy cabins. With the dense vegetation and uneven terrain, including a couple of bogs, the route couldn't possibly be straight. To keep our bearings, we made sure before tying each flag to a tree that we could look back and see the last one. About three-quarters of the way along, we were just about out of ribbon, so Ken stayed put while I advanced toward a hill within view. Within minutes, I intersected the existing trail to Mitchell Lake. We flagged this last stretch and returned to camp.

The following morning, we decided to go all the way through to the west end of Mitchell Lake, where the plane was to pick us up about 3 p.m. the day after and take us to our property. There would be less pressure if we pushed through in one day and camped overnight at the lake. Trail improvement would have to wait.

After eating breakfast, reorganizing our gear, and reassembling our packs, we set off. It was about 11 a.m. We romped across our bridge and forged up our flagged path. As might be expected according to Murphy's Law, about three-quarters of the way along, we couldn't find the next flag. Forty-five minutes later, we stumbled onto the old trail. The consolation was that Ken had found a better last-quarter route; the rub was that neither of us had the axe.

"You had it last," Ken insisted.

"I thought you had it last," I replied.

We eventually found the axe. Our spirits were up again, and the sun shone. From a new roll of ribbon, we flagged the better last stretch and then heavily flagged the vital point of intersection with the existing trail.

We started up the old Mitchell Lake trail about 2:30 p.m. The overgrowth indicated that it hadn't been traveled much since I had last been on it in 1980; it even disappeared in low, marshy places. Now even more deadfalls blocked the route, and there also seemed to be an increase in the number of streams crossing the trail.

When we reached the top of the trail shortly after 8 p.m., Mitchell Lake was still in daylight, a welcome change from previous ascents. We fished for supper along the short upper stretch of river and each caught a couple of trout. After a crudely cooked supper of beans and trout, Ken pitched his tent on a sloping ledge, then helped position the stashed, leaky canoe as a shelter for me.

We awoke the next morning to good weather and in good spirits. After a slim breakfast, we put our rods into action again. As 3 p.m. approached and then passed, I felt increasingly anxious about the prearranged pickup. Waiting for a late plane is tough for me to cope with quietly.

"Relax! He'll come," Ken reassured.

Not wanting to dampen his good mood, I moved around the south corner of the mouth to fish from the lakeshore. About 5:30 p.m., I hooked a nice-sized rainbow, but without enjoyment. That's how uneasy I was.

About 6:30 p.m., I returned dejectedly to the campsite and began to collect wood to cook a pathetically slim supper. Then I heard the plane. It was Gideon Schuetze. In his usual nonchalant, almost-amicable manner, he said something about Cariboo Days festivities having delayed him. Three and a half hours didn't matter now, as we taxied down the length of Mitchell Lake to the homestead.

Lined up on the shore to greet us were two father-and-son pairs: Gil and Greg Menzies and Bob and Dave Haslam. Ken and I climbed out of the plane with plenty of assistance and exchanged reports in high spirits. Gil admitted to having been about as anxious as I had been. After the other three flew out, Gil cooked a magnificent supper. Did Ken and I ever wolf it down!

The three of us enjoyed ten days of good weather, good grub, and good fishing. The dolly take, however, was nil; when Gil crowed about the twenty dollies that he and his mates had scored, I groused that they might have left a few for the trailblazers.

On the trip out, we couldn't find the start of the trail. It was mighty embarrassing as we fumbled around for about half an hour, especially after giving Gil such a sales pitch on our achievement. My error was directing the group toward the river too soon instead of leading them all the way up a small ridge. Making the correction, we finally got on the trail. Gil wasn't too impressed. I added flagging up and over the ridge for the next time. Then it was a breeze all the way down—at least Ken and I thought so.

Gil hardly said a word as he plodded along with a heavy backpack and his shotgun. I ribbed him (only once) that Greg had offered to take the shotgun out on the plane. When we got down to the tree bridge, Ken and I were keen to have Gil admire our engineering feat. Gil, however, was entirely intent on walking safely across it. He lightened up considerably when we arrived at the truck and a dry road.

The trail we had blazed was never used again. Attempting to use it the next summer, Pat O'Brien, Ken, and I were stymied at the Mitchell River crossing: our log bridge had been washed out of position. This gave us a true impression of the force of the current at high water, presumably in the spring. We each had the sense to immediately reject improvising another crossing. We returned to Williams Lake to charter a flight with Gideon. The alternative route was kaput.

CHAPTER SEVEN

Avalanched!

Each summer at Mitchell Lake brought new challenges. In 1985, Gil Menzies, colleague Jim Adams, and I were flown in by Mark Schuetze, Gideon's son. I helped unload the first couple of items and then, as usual and anxiously, I hotfooted it up the trail to check the cabin before the plane pulled out. On my third stride, I looked to the right and saw one squashed canoe. I had left it horizontal last year when hurriedly packing up to take a reduced-fare trip out a day earlier than scheduled. Well, I thought as I galloped on, that reduced fare cost us a canoe.

Nearing the site, I thought that I should be able to see the roof. In turning the last bend, I saw the cabin: it was down— pushed over—wrecked. It looked like a wounded moose, hip-shot and down unevenly on all fours with head sagging. I raced back to the shore to stop the unloading. What were we going to do?

"The cabin's wrecked," I blurted out, mouth dry and head half numb.

"What did it?" Gil reacted.

"I don't know. I didn't take time to look," I said.

"Well, let's decide what to do," suggested Gil, fairly composed.

I couldn't look at Jim. This was his first trip in, and he must have been wondering what he'd gotten himself into.

"Let's stay and rebuild," Gil valiantly added.

"Where? And with what equipment?" I inquired, mechanically.

"Why don't you check with your neighbors?" contributed Mark. "Verne Cooper, one of the owners, is there."

Determined to react positively rather than to cry and curse, I boated across to the Executive Lodge and confronted Verne, whom I had met just once before.

"Verne, I'm in a tight spot," I commenced as objectively as I could.

"Yes, we noticed. It must have been a slide," he replied sympathetically.

"We'll either have to pull out or try to rebuild," I said.

"Well, what do you need? You're welcome to stay in the utility cabin, and the toolshed is open. Help yourself to tools, nails, and whatever," he offered.

"Thank you!" I said with a great deal more feeling than I've ever said it before. Here's to Verne Cooper of Santa Rosa, California! He responded immediately, positively, and generously.

When I returned with the good word, Gil responded with alacrity. "We can do it! Relax, old buddy."

Good old Gil: this is what I could always expect of him. I started to unwind and feel well again. But what about Jim? He appeared to be in a state of wordless and stoical acquiescence.

On surveying the squashed canoe, now rated a minor mishap, I thought at first that a bear had been using it for a trampoline, but Mark assured us that an unusually heavy snowfall had been the culprit.

As Gil inspected the "wounded-moose" cabin, he pointed to the brush on the north side: it was bent in the same direction the building was skewed. The irrefutable conclusion was that an avalanche had done the cabin in.

Our consolation was that we could rebuild the cabin on the lakeshore, the logical site for a cabin, as the first cabin had served its purpose of establishing title to the property. We would haul as many logs and shakes as feasible from the old cabin down the trail to the new site. But what about our priceless little stove? All but the top was smashed or twisted, and we shed a couple of tears.

Mark readily agreed to return in a few days with spikes and tar paper. After he flew out, we unanimously agreed not to start the job until Monday. Did we ever have a task on our hands. And to think that Gil had planned to do some sketching during this sojourn!

We established ourselves at the neighbors' utility cabin, with a cooker improvised from parts of the wrecked stove erected on the beach in front. We fished that evening and all the next day. We still had our priorities straight. By Monday morning, we were gung ho to start the job.

We chose our landing point, just inside the northwest corner of the front lot, for the new site. Gil and Jim prescribed the following division of labor: while I prepared the new site, they would dismantle the cabin the first day and haul the usable materials the second day.

They lugged down the trail about a hundred logs (using foam-rubber pieces for shoulder cushioning), then several pieces of plywood, and finally many boxes of shakes. Each trip took five to ten minutes. I concentrated on clearing the site and cutting new perimeter joists, using the come-along to position them.

Some vertical posts and most of the rafters had to be replaced. On the third day, Gil had the bright idea of shortening the vertical corner posts a uniform few inches, enabling us to reuse these posts after cutting off their rotten bottom ends. Gil also sensibly insisted on increasing two small window openings to three larger ones.

Mark arrived on the sixth day with supplies and contributed some nimble help hoisting and installing the rafters.

For new shakes, we harvested more cedar. I was thankful to

be using Verne's Stihl chain saw, whose efficiency and lightness I appreciated.

Jim had become an adept and quick shake roofer, and one afternoon I couldn't split shakes fast enough to keep him supplied. Fuming, I finally switched from the splitter to the axe-head that I had used on the first cabin; the greater thickness of the axe-head forced an earlier split. I recovered a better mood, more like that of my two mates.

Gil and Jim were determined to finish by the middle of the second week in order to have three clear days for holidaying. Gil was intent on fishing the full extent of the lake, and Jim (just possibly) may have been contemplating some honest loafing.

What did we do other than build? Typically we labored until about 4 p.m. and then fished until about 9 p.m. or even 10 p.m., depending on when we could get Gil to quit. There was no question about humoring him: he cooked the late supper.

The weather was clear and hot. We enjoyed plunges into the lake every other day, with Jim the first one in and Gil the last. A few late evenings yielded breathtaking scenes, with the stars in bright array and the moon reflecting beautifully on rippling water.

As for the fishing, the shelf at our end of the lake wasn't very productive until Gil hit on fly-rod-with-sinking-line trolling. This method immediately revived the rainbow action, the lighter and vibrant fly rod making it more exciting than before. I had one electrifying grab by an enormous rainbow. It ran the line out, making the reel scream. When I stopped the reel too soon, the fish broke loose. The non-believers laugh when you report that the big ones get away. Little do they know.

We also enjoyed observing other wildlife, including two bald eagles, four curious and frisky squirrels, and one large porcupine that surprised me at our doorstep early one morning. We sighted only one bear—a small, spindly one—on the shore west of the Executive Lodge. In contrast to the scroungers of previous

After the avalanche

The second cabin

Inside the second cabin

summers, this bear had certainly been keeping its distance.

A week and a half into our stay, we completed the job of rebuilding. Making a small ceremony of it, we nailed up my name plate and took pictures.

"Here's to us. We did it!" Gil proclaimed.

"And here's to Verne Cooper, neighbor and gentleman!" I added.

Our two-week stay was quickly at an end. On our last day, we fished in the morning for take-home trout and then spent a busy five hours packing and securing. Mark Schuetze arrived on schedule, and we flew out shortly after 6 p.m.

We had restored the homestead, the challenge that faced us on arriving this time. My admiration for my two gritty buddies is enormous! Gil and I haven't managed to persuade Jim to return. (I wonder why.)

As Gil has often commented, if we had turned our back on the wrecked cabin and flown out, it would have been game over for us at Mitchell Lake. Not only do we still have a Mitchell home, but now it is an even better one. In forcing relocation to the lakeshore, the avalanche turned out to be a blessing.

CHAPTER EIGHT

The Neighbors

With the cabin resituated in 1985 to the lakeshore, our sojourns at Mitchell Lake have since been enriched in several ways.

With the open sky, day begins earlier and ends later. As the early morning sun breaks over the forest, its reflection from the snow-capped peaks diffuses the mist on the water. The wind from the west typically accelerates as morning advances, transforming the water from mirrorlike stillness to ripples and then to waves—raging waves, occasionally, that lash our shore; the lake returns to a peaceful stillness in late afternoon as the wind abates.

The transition from sunny and clear to overcast and stormy can be sudden and dramatic, with contending weather systems clashing overhead. And when storm is winning the battle, look out! If we happen to be out in the boat, we head rapidly for home or the closest shore to avoid getting soaked or running the risk of being overturned. Summer days are usually clear, warm, and pleasant—ideal for working, fishing, or loafing. A breeze reduces the insect nuisance.

We also see more of the neighbors at the Executive Lodge now that we're located on the lakeshore. I've gotten to know and like the regulars, especially Doug Tressler, construction veteran. My initial encounter with Doug was that first summer when he and Jim Harkey quizzed us on why we were building a cabin on what was soon to be their property.

When the Americans at the lodge occasionally had us over,

Doug would go on at some length about winters at Mitchell Lake and helicoptering over the adjacent valleys. I did a lot of listening, especially when he insisted that there were negotiable hiking trails to Christian Lake and from the East Mitchell River up to what we called the Twin Glacier. Gil Menzies and I wondered just how much hiking Doug had done, particularly after our own abortive hike to Christian Lake; we were later to revise our opinion.

One stormy day, Gil and I watched a boat inch its way from the west through heavy rain, finally pulling in to the neighbors' dock. Its three soaked passengers—Doug and two others—scampered into the Executive Lodge. The next morning, Doug invited us for coffee and told us the whole story.

Doug, his nephew, and one of his grandsons had started from Seattle, driven the Maeford Lake route, hiked in, and somehow crossed the Mitchell River (I should have quizzed him on this). They then hiked up the Mitchell Lake trail lugging an electric motor to power their boat stashed at the west end, but they had had to row when this motor failed. It had been a wet, rough trip, but they were dried out and in good form after a night's sleep. I was genuinely impressed with their feat.

"Doug, you're just as crazy as I've been," I said, seeing him now as a kindred spirit.

"Yeah, I suppose so," he grinned.

I guess Doug has come to respect us, too, for our perseverance. Egging us on to relate our experiences, he listens as much as he talks now. Amiable and generous, he has become a friend. His friendship was materially demonstrated when he persuaded Jim Harkey to give us a 9.5 horsepower boat motor in good working order for a paltry $150. They said they had been shaking their heads long enough about our puttering along with a measly four horsepower motor.

Gil returned one afternoon from fishing at the south corner of our end of the lake with news of visitors to the lake. He had noticed a boat and people setting up a camp on the delta, the flat extended shore on the other side of what we called the Dirty River (East Mitchell River). He had pulled in and met Betty Frank, guide and outfitter. She was directing a crew that was establishing a goat-hunting camp.

In checking this out the next day, I found no one home, but, sure enough, a cooking tent had been erected. They had probably boated back to the west end early that morning. I'd missed the visitors.

I finally met Betty Frank the next summer. While fishing one morning, Gil and I spotted somebody attempting to start the reluctant motor of an oversized boat at the west end. It was Betty Frank with her grandson. They had both hiked up the trail from her place near the north end of the North Arm of Quesnel Lake and were on their way to the camp on the delta. The next day, she would motor back to pick up her crew. Congenial and quick-talking, she gave the impression that wilderness hiking was child's play. What a woman! Gil got their motor started, and off they went.

The next day we were visited by Ray and Irene Stobie, Betty's crew, and their little girl. Easygoing and amiable, the Stobies had been employed to extend the camp facilities and cut hunting trails. We met them again that night at the Executive Lodge: it was Saturday night and the Americans were entertaining in grand style. Mitchell social life had really picked up. Betty, who had stayed home with the Stobies' child, was toasted "The Queen of the Cariboo." An amusing highlight of this party was listening to Ray, a local Métis, discuss family histories with a man from Idaho, who was also named Stobie. By the end of the evening, and with straight faces, the two Stobies had concluded that they were related.

Gil's interest in Mitchell Lake increased each summer, so when we decided we needed something that would provide more space and more shelter from the elements than the existing narrow cabin deck, Gil designed a gazebo, and together we built it.

It consists of log floor joists, vertical posts, partially open walls, a shake roof, and a sturdy floor of two-inch-thick cedar planks that I managed to produce using chalkline and a chain saw. Christened the "summer house," this gazebo is where we enjoy early morning coffee and work breaks, have brunch fairly regularly, and occasionally entertain neighbors.

Our best thinking percolates in the summer house over early morning coffee—boiled in pure water, cowboy style. On a wood-burning stove, boiling takes less time than percolating, and although Tom, my eldest son, has donated a complex, gadgety coffeemaker, we have still not used it. A symbol of what we try to avoid at our retreat, it remains at the bottom of a cardboard box. During the building of the summer house, Don Carter of Manitoba became a new neighbor in our corner of the east end. His log cottage, a precut package lifted in by helicopter, was erected immediately north of us. Don flies his own floatplane and seldom stays much more than a day or two at a time. As much as a retreat, his place seems to serve as a focal point for his flying jaunts.

After Don had his property fully surveyed, he confronted me with the disconcerting fact that our common boundary was a forty-five degree line from the shore, not a ninety degree one, which meant that three-quarters of our cabin was on his property. In relocating it after the avalanche, I sure slipped up on this. Much to my relief, he diplomatically asked me to move it "sometime."

Don engaged Ben Rauman, master log-builder of 100 Mile House, to improvise additional cottage and property features. In his early seventies, Ben maintains remarkable stamina; as a master craftsman, he possesses true ingenuity. I enjoyed listening to his unusual tales of being an immigrant in frontier Canada and a ski soldier fighting for Finland in World War II. His help would be invaluable in a future major building project.

The central figure in the Mitchell Lake scene is Gideon Schuetze, peerless bush pilot and proprietor of Sharp Wings Ltd., who took over Gale Fowler's flight service sometime after our 1979 sojourn. Standing over six feet tall, graying, muscular, and always bare-armed, he handles the various cargo items with energy and ease. His navigation doesn't require a map; he knows the whole of the Chilcoltin and Cariboo country like the back of his hand.

On one flight from Williams Lake, the North Arm of Quesnel Lake was so socked in that the flight line up the valley to Mitchell Lake was not visible. Gideon landed on a small lower lake to wait for some clearing. A couple of hours later, he was apparently able to see (we certainly couldn't) an opening at the top of the valley, and we proceeded at minimal altitude, safely and successfully.

When we've had somebody new with us on the flight in, Gideon has put on the little act where he closes his eyes for a bit and then after arrival says, "That was sure a nice nap I had."

If there's a problem at Mitchell Lake and he's in the vicinity, it's Gideon to the rescue. One time, a couple of greenhorn guests at the Northern Lights Lodge were caught out in a storm; their boat overturned and sank, but they were close enough to shore that they were able to land themselves. Gideon improvised a grappling hook out of bent spikes, then raised and recovered the boat.

The service expected of him is incredibly diverse. His schedule is often derailed, but he takes everything in stride and usually with a smile. His brand of humor is inimitable. It includes what we term gideosyncracies: for example, "You need windows? Make your own—there's lots of sand here." One time he flew a couple of German hikers into the delta south of us. When we later asked him how far and for how long they hiked, he replied, "I don't know. I haven't seen them since."

Since three of us were defeated at the lower Mitchell River in

1984, I have been fully content to fly with Gideon. The logisitics of non-air travel are just too difficult. We had only limited success stashing our boat and motor at the west end of Mitchell Lake one winter. A falling tree missed by inches crushing the boat, and the little house for the motor slid halfway down the bank. It is only practical to arrive via Mitchell River if there is already someone at our place on the east end of Mitchell Lake who will boat to the west end to pick up the intrepid second-comers.

My son Ken and his friend Darrin Belak did the paddle-hike trip from Lowry's Lodge on Quesnel Lake in 1987, when Gil and I were in residence and able to pick them up. They found it a worthwhile experience, one that I'd like to enjoy once more. But for transporting ourselves and supplies, it is Gideon we rely on. He is dependable and fair, and, when timing permits, he gives us the benefit of flight cost-sharing with the neighbors.

One bright day we were working around the place when a boat from the Northern Lights Lodge came along with a friendly couple aboard. They seemed interested in meeting us, so we invited them ashore for cool tea and a look at our simple abode.

"It's like an old trapper's cabin, isn't it?" Gil enthused.

"Yes, it is," the husband replied warmly but rather vacantly. A half hour after they had left to resume fishing, a second Northern Lights boat approached.

"Hello! Can you tell me what kind of a fish this is?" the fellow inquired.

After they pulled up, we readily identified it as a Dolly Varden.

In the ensuing conversation, it became apparent that he had known darn well that it was a dolly; the first couple had told them about us, and they wanted to see for themselves. Gil and I were established as the local curiosities. Looking at our grizzled beards and battered Stetsons, they probably thought, at least initially, that we were full-time hermits. We love the role.

CHAPTER NINE

An Obsession
and a Plan

Gil Menzies and I were fishing one fine day at the west end of Mitchell Lake. I made a good cast from a big rock; the spinner (Len Thompson red/white #8, of course) dropped three-quarters of the way across in the fast water. The fish hit it immediately and took off, downstream and deep, with that heavy "dolly" pull. With the rod butt tucked into my tummy to reduce the arm work, I let the line run out. But I had to start reeling in soon, before the dolly got farther downstream in the faster current. I reeled; it ran; I reeled—it ran again. To bring the fish in up the middle and out from the submerged logs closer in, I wobblingly eased myself off the rock and out into the water.

"Keep cool," I muttered, trying intently to keep the rod tip up and plant my feet on smaller, non-slippery underwater boulders.

Just as I was starting to gain on the fish, the line abruptly seized. I could no longer crank the reel. There was no retrieve whatsoever.

It's snagged the line around a log, I said to myself. To Gil I shouted: "Gil! I've got a good one, but I can't budge it. Can you help? I don't want to lose it."

"Hold on. I'm coming with the net," Gil shouted back. He'd been fishing at the mouth, thirty yards upstream from me. Within seconds, he came around the willows, plodding carefully through the water. Good old Gil.

"Where is it? Can you see it?" he asked.

"I can't get out to where it's snagged. The water's too deep. Could we use the boat? Could you float me out in the boat with the rope from the bow? I know it wouldn't be safe to start the motor."

Within another hundred yards downstream, the river becomes a frothing cataract as it descends the valley to the lower lake. A miscue with the four horsepower motor would result in losing control of the boat—potential for disaster.

"I'll get the boat. I just hope the lousy rope is long enough. Hold on!"

I was holding on all right, but by this time the dolly (it had to be a dolly) could well have broken free on the other side of the snag. Within minutes Gil returned with the boat. I one-handedly pulled myself into the stern and kept the rod tip up, as Gil repeatedly reminded me.

"How's your footing, Gil? Make sure your footing is good!" I was worried that he would slip: despite all his fishing experience, he hadn't logged as many miles as I had floundering up and down rivers in waders. Was this dolly—if it was still hooked—worth one or both of us drowning?

With Gil paying out the rope, the boat promptly floated backward downstream a few feet, then stopped. I wasn't close enough to see the snag.

"More rope!" I ordered.

"That's it. There isn't any more. Why didn't you put in a longer rope before we left?"

Ignoring this poorly timed but clearly relevant question, I reeled in the slack line. I was still two yards short of the snag.

"Can you see it?" Gil asked impatiently.

"I'm looking. I'm looking."

With the rod butt still jammed against my torso, I held the rod tip up, clumsily grabbed a paddle with my left hand, and managed to push the boat out a bit more. It was enough. The line slackened, and I spotted the dolly's snout under a log. There was movement at the other end of the line.

"It's still on. It's free of the log," I hollered.

"Keep your tip up, Bill! I'm pulling the boat back. Reel it in! When you get it where we can see it, I'll use the net."

"Great! Great!" I jabbered with some relief. "It's coming, and it's tired. I can see it. It's starting to turn belly up. Must be seven or eight pounds."

Gil deftly netted the fish, and, with the immediate release of line tension, the hook popped out of its mouth. We emerged on shore intact, wetter with sweat, thank goodness, than with river water.

That thirty-five-minute episode netted us a prime dolly, seven pounds, minimum. So who's to argue? The fish had been smart enough to shove its head under a log that was firmly anchored close to the bottom and perpendicular to the shoreline. The line had curved over, down, and partly under the log. Any pull on that line was against the log. When the boat and rod tip extended far enough to free the line, the pull on the line then switched from log to fish.

This two-man victory had depended on cooperation, trust, and that darn-fool determination to "get the big one in." We recounted it over and over back at the cabin with a supper of dolly steaks.

"You were worried I was going to let go of the boat and send you cruising down the cataract to your death, weren't you?" Gil joshed.

"No," I replied with a fairly straight face. "I just didn't want you to fall in, sprain something, and not be able to cook supper."

Now that we have a lighter aluminum boat and a 9.5 horsepower motor, a round trip the length of Mitchell Lake to our choice fishing spots can be made without any hurry in half a day rather than a full day. In addition to the west end, our choice spots are some of the creek mouths, which we have named over the years: on the south shore, Twin Creek, Dolly Creek, Staircase Creek, and Osprey Creek; and on the north shore, Gideon's Creek and Bucko Creek.

Dolly Creek (the Executive Lodge Americans call it Four-Mile Creek) is the very best spot to fish from shore, enjoy lunch, and snooze when the action momentarily subsides. We named it Dolly Creek some time ago because this is where we've landed—and not landed—some of the best dollies. It has the greatest flow of the Mitchell creeks because it drains down a deep ravine from the largest of the glaciers above. The open terrain on shore affords the creek mouth full sun.

Often when just Gil and I arrive, it's a bit of a race to see who makes the first parallel, close-to-shore cast, a cast that often scores a dolly in the first couple of minutes. I once connected with one that could have been a ten-pounder: we saw it roll above the surface only once in the thirty-minute bout. Initially, I varied the reel tension quite deftly but couldn't gain on it as it surged down and away. Finally, the fish raced toward the fast water, then back, then straight out into the lake with "all jets turned on." The line went limp as it made off to freedom. I saluted that dolly with a right hand that would remain partially numb for the next five days.

Once Gil lost a dolly when the line broke at the spinner. Three days later, he caught the same dolly at Americans' Creek, more than four miles distant, and was able to recover his lost spinner.

Just before leaving Dolly Creek in the late afternoon, I often make a long cast to the west; the spinner lands, sending a splash of silver across the sun's path.

During a lull in the action on one of these fishing tours, Gil and I got onto the subject of building a new cabin.

"Cedar. Vertical half-logs. Would be great, eh?" I enthused.

"I suppose. It should be three or four times larger with a couple of separate bedrooms. And you need a proper foundation, like cement piers," Gil suggested.

"We'll need help. How are we going to get a crew in here?" I countered.

"Extra hands are needed to raise the rafters, but the alternative would be to spend some money on a hoist system," my buddy blithely continued.

"Hey, wait a minute! This is going to cost hundreds. Maybe I should check with Fred Brooks about subdividing to raise some capital," I said, thoughtfully and innocently.

"Be sure to check with me before you do that. I might be able to get into the act. Anyway, let's start sketching a plan," Gil said, equally thoughtful.

I wondered briefly how serious Gil was about "getting into the act." It was obvious that Mitchell Lake had just as tenacious a hold on him as it did on me. We were individually obsessed. Whereas I talked whimsically about how my dad would have enjoyed this place if he were alive, Gil rhapsodized about establishing a retreat for his progeny. But how did his obsession translate in terms of an investment? He didn't mention it again during this trip. We did, however, work up some design ideas.

CHAPTER TEN

One Log at a Time

When asked how he built a log house, an old bush carpenter replied, "One log at a time." There is more truth than humor in this answer, as Gil Menzies and I found out. When building a log house from scratch in a wilderness location, one has to be ready to make changes, to improvise, and to be creative. A building strategy is necessary but cannot be "etched in wood."

During the winter of 1989, Fred Brooks legally transferred his half share in the Mitchell Lake property to Gil. Gil's participation was now enthusiasm plus dollars and gave impetus to building a new house. I wanted to do another vertical, half-log exterior, this time with cedar instead of spruce. Cedar ripped easily, peeled readily, and had an attractive light color. Gil was specific about the structure's size, foundation, windows, and position for the best view.

By the summer of 1989, we had the site selected, blueprints in hand, and a stockpile of seven-foot cedar half-logs that I had started to harvest and rip the summer before. The site was several yards south of the summer house; the new house would front on the shore of the lake. Gil designed and drafted the plan: a twenty-five-foot by thirty-foot area, two bedrooms, a common room (living room and kitchen), an inset deck, and a gable roof with a one-to-two pitch.

My son Tom and his son Robbie, aged eleven, flew in to Mitchell Lake with me in early July for ten days that summer, before Gil's arrival. Thanks to boy-scout training, my grandson was able to adapt to a primitive experience that would be "awesome" for any suburban kid. Although he seemed to enjoy catching his first and second trout, what he really got a kick out of was running the boat motor. He became so adept that he could easily yank the heavy 9.5 horsepower motor up and out of the water in those critical couple of seconds before hitting the beach.

It was Tom's second sojourn at Mitchell Lake, and he again proved to be a thoughtful, innovative helper as well as a darn good cook. I don't know what I'll do if I ever run out of good cooks. Tom particularly impressed me by being a more cheerful and attentive dad than I had ever been.

We were fully equipped with three chain saws: to our veteran Husqvarna with sixteen-inch bar, we had added a 034AV Stihl with sixteen-inch bar and a 2101XP Husqvarna with twenty-four-inch bar. The large Husqy was purchased mainly for using with the Alaska mill; the Stihl would be our general utility saw; the small Husqy would be used mainly for ripping and trimming cedar logs.

In felling one cedar that was about three and a half feet in diameter at the base, I held the large Husqy above shoulder height to reach the reduced diameter higher up the tree. The weight of the saw made this already strenuous and precarious maneuver dangerous when the tree went down in the opposite direction intended—without mishap, thank goodness. I resolved to restrict myself to harvesting trees of fewer than three feet in base diameter.

With Tom's help I felled cedars and cut them into seven-foot lengths. We peeled a lengthwise strip of bark from each log, established the midpoint at each end, and chalklined the length. Then we ripsawed each log into lengthwise halves and completed the peeling. Tom and I lugged these exterior wall half-logs to the building site. I then grouped them face down in fours or fives with ends alternating, pressed them tightly together with a crowbar inserted in the ground, and ran the ripsaw through the seams to make a snug fit. We then started stockpiling these half-logs, though farther back from the front of the site than I thought necessary.

On my son and my grandson's last day, Tom caught five rainbow while trolling his sinking-fly line with Robbie manning the motor. Later, Gideon delivered Gil, Darrin Belak, and my son Ken, taking Tom and Robbie with him when he flew out again. That evening Gil reinstated himself as head chef, serving up superb T-bone steaks, mushrooms, and corn-on-the-cob prepared on his outdoor stove.

With a four-man crew, the chips really flew for a week or so. We established the house perimeter, leaving several yards between the shore and the house in order to have something of a front yard. The back line of the house ran only about three feet in front of the stockpile of exterior wall half-logs! Tom's foresight regarding the half-logs had proved to be better than mine.

In clearing the site, we thought it wise to eliminate an ancient, barkless cedar to the right of the half-log stockpile because there was no way of knowing how secure its roots were. (We all remembered the tree that was uprooted one night in 1978.) The trunk of the old cedar was about three and a half feet in diameter. I was determined to make the cutting easier by doing it ten feet up, where the diameter was a foot less.

I improvised a platform with a cleat nailed to the cedar itself and a second cleat nailed to a neighboring tree to support a horizontal plank. I positioned the front gouge cut to cause the cedar to fall east. To minimize my risk upon completing the back cut, I would speedily hand the chain saw down to a crew member (I can't remember who volunteered) and scamper down the ladder as the tree creaked and slowly toppled.

That was the plan.

The reality was that the cedar fell a bit to the left of the prescribed location and on the way down grazed a corner of the plank. The plank shivered ever so slightly. I didn't make a move and was immensely relieved when the plank stilled. I began to breathe normally once again, and my crew members applauded spiritedly.

"Yea Dad!" "Yea mighty woodsman!"

"Thank you, thank you," I replied, bowing immodestly. What a sixty-four-year-old grandstander I was!

We celebrated the squeaky success by going fishing for the rest of the afternoon.

During the next week, Ken and Darrin lugged more cedar half-logs from the northeast harvesting location to the building site. Close by, I felled spruces that were one to two feet in diameter and seventy to ninety feet tall. I cut them into lengths of twenty-five and thirty feet. These we moved with a come-along onto the site, where Ken and Darrin laboriously removed the bark with machetes. The larger spruces would serve as sill beams; the smaller ones were reserved for rafters.

Gil concentrated mainly on locating and digging holes for the sixteen foundation piers. In performing the initial survey, he had hoped the holes would not coincide with stumps, but four of them did. Using a chain saw, I helped cut the roots of the stumps out. Cutting below ground level is the very worst use of saw chains; fortunately, I could afford to waste one. Gil then hauled rocks to fill the holes in preparation for the concrete.

We took a day to relax before Ken and Darrin had to leave. Gil and Darrin fished the shelf and Americans Creek. Gil hooked a huge dolly in the dorsal fin, making the retrieval tricky and lengthy. It was a nine-pound contender in a forty-five-minute bout!

Meanwhile, Ken and I relaxed in the summer house, watched

the resident bald eagle soar and dip for a few minutes, and then had a heart-to-heart natter. I had been fussing about procedures for chores such as fetching water and washing dishes.

"Can I use a little of my own initiative?" Ken asked.

"Of course. It's just that I find it easier to stick to a set routine, and then I don't have to think about what I'm doing. But let's try to help each other enjoy this place. Otherwise, there isn't a lot of sense in being here, is there?"

"Agreed," he concluded.

The next morning, Ken and Darrin left Mitchell Lake. As they boarded the plane, we told them we had enjoyed their company and appreciated their hard work.

Gil and I put in eleven and a half hours one day moving the top sections of felled spruces from the lake up to the site with a come-along and peeling them, then completing the stockpiling of rafters. We thankfully took a break when the plane delivered gas, three bags of cement, and one sauna tube. Later, while Gil was having a dickens of a time cutting the sauna tube into sixteen small sections (until he borrowed Ben's handsaw), I cleared a wheelbarrow route from shore to site.

The following building day was the longest—thirteen hours. That was the day we manufactured the sixteen cement foundation piers. We were obsessed with finishing the cement work in one day in order to avoid repeating the startup and cleanup.

Fifty times, we mixed cement and sand and water. Forty-nine times, Gil pushed the wheelbarrow load from the beach up the circuitous route to the site. I gladly yielded to Gil's superior strength. Carrying shovels up to the site, helping mix cement, and filling holes were strenuous enough for me. He did permit me to push the last half wheelbarrow load.

Midway through filling each hole to the top of its six-inch-high sauna tube piece, Gil fussed about the cement not setting up properly. He borrowed a fourth bag of cement from Ben and then worked like a maniac so that we could finish the job in the one day. What a day! What an accomplishment!

During the next couple of days, we calculated heights for the cedar posts and positioned them on the sixteen cement piers. Sure we were working hard, but we were both passionately committed.

What contributed to this passion? A warm, moonlit night, for one thing. One night when the moon rose in the south, it appeared only partly at first, with cloud sailing by in front of it. It then emerged fully round and brilliant, laying a shimmering path of light across the water. Above the south shore, the peaks and patches of snow glistened against the black sky. On our shore, the boats and recently towed logs appeared as clearly as in daylight.

Early morning could also be exhilarating. One morning from the summer house, I watched the sky brighten with the sunrise. The only sounds were a squawking crow and the hum of the creek in our north corner. Near shore, the lake's surface shimmered in the gentle breeze and early light; beyond, the water was mirror-calm. About four feet from shore, a rainbow hopped-skipped in pursuit of a fly. What a morning! When I am close to such beauty, I'm inclined to believe there must be a greater power.

The good thing about leaving Mitchell at the end of July in 1989 was that we would return in a month. It would be our first September at Mitchell. Realizing that our momentum would be interrupted by only a month instead of a whole winter, we happily planned the next building phase: the raising of the sill beams into position on top of the pier logs. For this we needed a fairly complex hoist system, which was now taking shape in Gil's noggin. And I was making headway in convincing him that we could use our Alaska mill to make the two-inch by eight-inch floor joists from the splentiful spruce surrounding the site. So it was three cheers for a September resumption.

CHAPTER ELEVEN

The First September

On September 6, 1989, Gil Menzies and I were back at Mitchell Lake. The insect nuisance was diminished by colder nights, and the weather was perfect for the first job at hand: installing a 1500-pound-capacity hoist system for lifting the sill beams and the rafters into position.

We picked three spar trees, one near each of the two front corners of the house perimeter and the third just behind the center of the back line. It was a challenge to climb the twenty-five feet up each tree to affix the cable supports. For this feat, I improvised a safety belt from a four-foot length of high-quality rope and two boat snap-buckles. Our primitive ten-foot ladder put me into position to hammer into the trunk and then climb a series of twelve-inch spikes, taking me to a height of twenty-five feet. Thanks to the safety belt, I was able to climb each spar tree without too much strain. Gil then lag-screwed a boat-winch to the back spar tree and connected it by cable to the overhead system to keep it taut when loaded.

Although the system hoisted and positioned the sill beams well, the weight of the beams caused the three spar trees to bend inward. We remedied this somewhat by attaching support cables to three additional trees. And that was Gil's hoist system designed to replace a squad of men.

Gil and I began each day by reviewing the building plan to determine the work for the day. If we had different opinions about how something should be done, we talked it out. Invariably, one would persuade the other. Or we would strike a compromise. If Gil knew more about the topic of discussion (the plan or the hoist system, for example), my need to understand prompted me to quiz him in minute detail, which led to his clarifying or extending his own thinking. The same process occurred when he questioned me about the chainsawing.

We reached early agreement on the seating of the exterior logs on the sill beams. These half-logs would be set in tight vertical rows that would tightly abut two-inch by twelve-inch by nineteen-foot ledgers. The ledgers would largely eliminate floor drafts and mouse access.

In beginning with the subfloor structure, I flattened the inside edges of the sill beams using the small Husqy and a sharp ripsaw chain, and Gil levelled the tops of the beams with an axe. We then selected and felled a nearby spruce for making the ledgers.

Gil cleared passageways on both sides of the downed spruce while I prepared the large Husqy for insertion into the Alaska mill frame. After we had delimbed the spruce and cut it into nineteen-foot lengths, Ben Rauman came over from the Executive Lodge and helped outline cuts on the ends of the pieces for doing the de-slabbing. The tough part of squaring off the spruce pieces was positioning Ben's fourteen-foot starting board. The board had to be shimmed as precisely as possible to compensate for the tapering diameter of the pieces, and because the board was five feet shorter than our planned ledger pieces, this reshimming had to be done partway through each of the three slab cuts for each log. All of this demanded time and patience. Using the too-short starting board was just a challenge we would have to struggle with until we could mill a longer and truer one. (Remember, there wasn't a lumber yard handy.)

We eventually managed to de-slab each piece and then slice off adequate ledger planks. We'd made the big start on Alaska milling. One not-so-trivial trick I discovered to reduce the push-force needed was propping up a piece with one end higher than the other and running the saw from the high end on a downhill grade.

After completing the milling of the ledgers, we began to mill two-inch by eight-inch floor joists. Setting up the starting board for each joist was intensely demanding. After changing the saw's chain late one afternoon, I clumsily struggled with the reinsertion of the saw into the mill. Overly tired and frustrated at not having a third hand, I lost my cool. Gil was not impressed with my behavior. I decided I would try a midday "power nap" the next day to help reduce my stress level.

From the summer house the next morning, I admired a jay with a handsome crested head and navy blue body as it flitted and pecked on the shore. This jay was darker than its Alberta cousin, and I later found out that it was a Steller's jay.

The squirrels were not as admirable. They were snatching our work gloves. We finally cottoned on when the fourth and fifth ones went missing. I discovered one morning that my carpenter's pouch had been pulled off the table in the summer house, dragged halfway across the floor, and emptied of the work gloves. We supposed the gloves were ideal for nest building.

I found myself awake at 4 a.m. on September 15, so I went out. It was a beautiful moonlit night. I built a driftwood fire on the beach and sat near it contentedly. Sparks from the fire drifted out over the lake. Pinpoints of light danced like fireflies on the water.

I thought about our freedom at Mitchell Lake, about the absence of human-imposed restrictions. Maybe this freedom to act unhindered represents an ideal reality; maybe this is how the next existence will be. And I just might be ready for it, I thought, now that I'm more more attuned to nature than I have ever been—if this is a prerequisite.

When day finally dawned, I noticed new snow on the higher peaks.

The daytime reality was installing ledgers. We had a battle with an extremely heavy ledger that was close to three inches thick and loaded with sap. Striving to keep the ledger level while jockeying its dead weight into true position, Gil worked up a lather. He also neglected to exert leg and hip force and wrenched his back. This shut us down at noon.

We were awakened from that afternoon's nap by a boat; it was Betty Frank arriving with a hunting client, a young man from Pennsylvania. He commented on how difficult it was to keep up to Betty's galloping hiking pace. When Betty casually mentioned a coffee shortage, we happily contributed half a pound; when we casually mentioned a chain oil shortage, she promptly said she could help with that and later delivered a bottle of chain oil.

Next day, Gil's bad back slowed him down considerably, so I tried to keep a jump ahead of him to do any necessary lifting. We continued work by putting spacers between the floor joists, but we were spending less time than before on the project so that Gil could recuperate. With this shorter workday, we read more. Gil was enjoying Michener's *Journey*; I was making a start on his *Alaska*.

When the floor framework was finished, we went ahead with wall construction: first cutting, peeling, and erecting the whole-log corner posts, then positioning milled plates horizontally on top of the posts. These plates were only fourteen feet long, the length of the starter board, so they had to be lap-jointed. Making the cuts for these joints was difficult.

After completing the horizontal plates, Gil and I were both uneasy about how low the front roofline was going to be. It would limit the view from the deck. We voiced our concern the next morning in the summer house, but we were so unwilling to tear down and rebuild that we rationalized. We naively agreed that

The author anchoring the hoist system, twenty-five feet up

Finishing the front wedge cut in order to fell a large cedar

Gil hoisting the front beam into position

Ken and the author in front of the gazebo called the summer house

The author at work

Adventures at Mitchell Lake

Arriving in Gideon's Cessna

Robbie standing on a felled cedar

Towing cedar logs from the south shore

Bucko with a good catch

we could insert a large skylight low in the roof toward the front of the house in order to compensate for the low roofline.

We resolutely pressed on with the installation of the vertical exterior logs. We started with the back (east) wall, hoping our workmanship would improve by the time we got to the front. I cut the half-logs to length and fitted them into the rectangular frame made by the posts, ledgers, and plates. When I needed him, Gil helped with holding and nailing, but he worked mainly on debranching and peeling newly felled trees for the pieces to be placed above the plates.

The good weather continued, and we felt fully blessed one evening while we sat on the beach admiring the golden foliage of the south-shore deciduous trees aglow in the setting sun. Above Christian Valley to the south, a white strip of jet-plane vapor stretched across the sky. Having observed the strip before, we concluded that this must be a regular route.

On September 22, which happens to be my dad's birthday, we skipped fishing and had a relatively early supper. Dolly, barbe-cued whole on the beach cooker, served with boiled spuds and creamed asparagus, made a pleasant change from a fried supper. Afterward, we sat out in the warm, clear evening sipping hot chocolate and munching cookies until the stars emerged brightly above the black outline of the mountains.

Having finished the east wall, I began work on the south wall, and Gil started applying Javex to the wall logs to remove mildew preparatory to oiling them. We were both working hard when a helicopter arrived at the Executive Lodge. Soon after hollering greetings, Jim Harkey, Doug Tressler, and his brother Gary came across to inspect our project. They were generally impressed.

"Do you think this roofline is high enough?" inquired Jim, who is about six feet two inches tall. "And will the doorway be high enough?" he added as he stood in the door space and had to scrunch his head down.

"Doubtful, eh?" Gil replied.

Jim's questions heightened the dissatisfaction Gil and I had been repressing about the low roofline.

The Executive Lodge fellows insisted on having us over that evening for fried chicken and beans. Our bellies comfortably filled, we got a kick out of their enthusiasm for our project and their several suggestions regarding structural strengthening. It was pitch-black when we left to cross the water to our place, so we could not see a thing on our shoreline. We had to laugh at ourselves the next morning when we saw how far south we had beached the boat.

Our neighbors returned the next morning to report how things looked from up above. Earlier that morning they had flown south over Christian Valley, east over Twin Falls, then north about fifteen miles toward Bowron Lake. On the way back, they landed on what they called Strawberry Meadow to stretch their legs and sample the abundant wild strawberries. While Doug was recounting most of this, Jim nosed around our building project. Maybe someday Jim will invite us to go on one of these upper-level jaunts.

As I progressed clockwise from east to north building the walls, Gil continued diligently with the Javex and the Naturoil. We were pleased with both the outer appearance and the inner, sawed-face appearance of the walls.

Before I got very far with the north wall, more cedar had to be harvested. I zeroed in on a huge cedar in the northeast area of our property and managed another strenuous felling operation. I was again cutting with the heavy Husqy above my shoulders where the tree's diameter was less. Although the tree fell in the prescribed direction, I was arm-weary and resolved (again!) never to cut above the hip.

After debranching and cutting the cedar into seventy-four-inch sections, I made the revolting discovery that cedar does not peel easily in September because of the sap. Live and learn. Of course, Ben Rauman could have told us that the peeling should have been done before August. We would use this cedar later for furniture and would finish the north wall the following summer with other cedar.

Something else I learned that fall was that I can't sit in a boat without almost freezing to death after the October sun drops down. On our fourth to last day, we fished Dolly Creek and the west end. Although the sun shone, the down draft at Dolly Creek was cold, so we crossed to the warmer north shore. After the sun had gone down, I became chilled without realizing it. By the time we got home shortly after 6 p.m., I was vibrating with chill and burrowed into my sleeping bag. Gil served me hot soup in bed, and I finally began to warm up. I'll kid him forever, though, for leaving the dishes for me to do the next day when I had recovered from what we guessed was mild hypothermia. That ended the boat fishing for the season, and it was fishing from the shore for the remainder of the sojourn.

We did have a few chores for the last few days: milling seven-inch by five-inch load-bearing beams, harvesting and stockpiling rafters and internal wall logs, and cleaning up and burning debris. Using the hoist system, we installed the sturdy, load-bearing beams. In so doing, we achieved two worthwhile results: the minor achievement was eliminating two lap-jointed plates that I hadn't been happy with; the major correction was raising the front roofline ten inches. The roofline problem that had been gnawing away at us was solved. We rejoiced!

CHAPTER TWELVE

Bucko

Kervyne LaRoque—outdoorsman, resource officer, carpenter, teacher—went in to Mitchell Lake with me in July 1990. His know-how, initiative, and enthusiasm notably contributed to the Mitchell experience. What else would you expect from a Manitoba farm boy? And he was a good cook. Again, I was lucky.

The fishing was better than ever, the north-shore creek mouths being as dynamic as those on the south shore. On our first tour, we had a terrific time. The trout responded to almost every cast, or so it seems now. Each time he got a hit, Kervyne emitted a "Yippee" so I renamed him Bucko.

In fishing Twin Creek, Dolly Creek, and Osprey Creek on the way to the west end, the response was so good that we readily agreed on a minimum "keeper" size. And I was prompted to use for the first time the Len Thompson barbless spinner that I had been procrastinating about for the past few seasons.

I was rewarded at the west end of the lake with the capture of two rainbow, each close to two pounds. Bucko assisted in netting the first one; the second one, I managed to bring in by myself. I worked the rainbow carefully over a submerged log with tentacle-like branches; I held the rod high and adjusted the reel tension with some deftness. I was immodestly pleased to have used the barbless spinner—a minor conservational effort.

The most memorable moment of that day occurred east of the Northern Lights Lodge at a north-shore creek I subsequently named Bucko Creek. When Bucko hooked a medium-sized rainbow, a second, especially large fish hit the same line almost instantaneously, pulling heavily and plunging to the bottom. Undoubtedly a dolly. Eventually, on the retrieve, we saw that it was in fact a dolly (probably about five pounds). It approached the surface with the rainbow in its mouth.

"It must have jawed right through the rainbow to be hooked," I suggested.

"Or the line is snagged around it," Bucko countered. "But we've got to have a picture. Get the camera out of my bag."

"OK, let it run a bit. I've got to have the net ready as well."

A few more seconds elapsed as I waited for the dolly to come right up to the surface so that it would show in the picture. Once more it jerked hard against Bucko and then drove straight out from the boat unattached. It had simply let go of the rainbow. It hadn't been hooked or snagged; that greedy son-of-a-gun had tenaciously hung on with jaw and fin until it decided to quit. I unhooked the mauled rainbow, threw it after the departing dolly and hollered, "You earned it!"

Bucko's experience as a hunter and as a resource officer in northern Saskatchewan made him a useful mate for the Mitchell retreat. He got on well with Ben Rauman too. And Bucko upgraded my performance in pouring white gas into the lantern and in draining the aluminum boat. I had no idea that the former was possible without spilling. What you do is tilt the top of the can so that the aperture is on the high side, then pour. And a leaky boat needs less bailing if you remove the drain plug while traveling (being careful not to drop it overboard) and re-insert it before slowing to stop.

Bucko was greatly helpful in the business of harvesting cedar on the south shore. The trick to felling each tree was to take maximum advantage of the downward slope, which, unfortunately, bottomed out a few yards short of the shore. After being felled, the logs were cut into two sections, then delimbed and peeled. Where the slope was insufficient, Bucko used roller logs to move the logs. With crowbar in hand, he pried here and lifted there. Half the time, I was slipping and lurching because I couldn't get any boot traction. I've never been more willing to relinquish seniority in favor of youth and energy. On a couple of holdups we had to use a come-along, but eventually we managed to propel four lengths of prime cedar into the water.

Before rigging up for the towing, we took a break. Torn between fishing and a plunge, Bucko combined the two with some casts in his birthday suit. The towing went smoothly in two trips, and we now had enough cedar to finish the exterior north wall.

In talking up the Mitchell experience before leaving Calgary, I had offered to take Bucko on a hike. So on a good-weather day we headed east up the East Mitchell River on one of Betty Frank's trails. We were stymied a couple of times at old avalanche clearings because of bush density and water. While I stayed put at the end of the path, Bucko would make a loop to look for its continuation. He maintained his usual cheerfulness throughout the hike, except when he barged into a nest of ill-tempered wasps. He hollered angrily and rapidly reversed direction but did get zapped on the tummy.

We proceeded to an open stretch of riverbank, a good viewing spot. Through the binoculars we saw the magnificent Twin Falls a couple of miles away. Along the falls' south wall, water ran out of a tunnel. Continuing up the river a mile or so, we saw what appeared to be a beaver dam and pond. We didn't see any animals, but bear and moose droppings were evident.

About four hours later, we got back to the lake. We'd hiked upriver about five sweaty miles—far enough on a hot day.

One morning I opened the door at 4:45 a.m. to check the weather and looked up into the face of a big black bear. It was standing right there on the doorstep. I gulped and squeaked, "Bear!" Also surprised, the bear turned and ambled toward the shore. Stopping abruptly, it came back a few steps and fixed me with a penetrating gaze. The sad, elongated face vaguely reminded me of a teacher I had had half a century before. My visage didn't excite the bear either; it turned to the shore and took off. We didn't see it again.

"If I had this place, I would do one thing differently," Bucko wryly said to me on his second-to-last day. "I wouldn't work as hard as you do."

I think either he had his tongue in cheek or he meant "I wouldn't work as slowly as you do." Perhaps ironically, he then busied himself with clearing our beachfront: removing driftwood, cutting out alder and piling and burning. He slaved in the heat that day and through the next day until well past 6 p.m., when Gideon Schuetze arrived (hours late) to drop off Gil Menzies and pick up Bucko. I was impressed with the way Bucko kept working instead of stewing impatiently while waiting for the plane. He had had previous experience with behind-schedule plane service in remote areas.

Here's to Bucko! He made his mark at Mitchell.

CHAPTER THIRTEEN

To Close
Before Winter

During the middle two weeks of July 1990, Gil Menzies and I continued to build the new house at Mitchell Lake. We had decided to replace the starter board method of Alaska milling with the Granberg mill rail method. The Granberg mill rail consisted of a bracket kit and two sixteen-foot-long fir two-by-fours. This method was to be a decided improvement on the starter board method because it would enable us to produce truer pieces with minimal exasperation.

We remounted the hoist system, milled and installed the remaining five-inch by seven-inch beams, installed the whole-log inner walls, and, under Ben Rauman's direction, harvested more cedar from the south shore.

In September, we would return with plans to hoist and install the seven rafters and work on the roof and gables until we had the house closed in for winter.

When September came, we drove Gil's three-quarter-ton truck, loaded with windows, to Gideon Schuetze's floatplane base at Williams Lake. We arrived on September 11 to find that the Beaver we had ordered had been held over at another lake and that the Cessna was undergoing repair. Gideon offered two options: we could wait a day or two for the return of the Beaver; or he would ask a friend to fly us in right away, and Gideon would fly in the windows and plywood for the gables within a few days. Waiting in Williams Lake had little appeal, so it was an easy choice.

And thus we met Tex Fosberry—contractor, hobbyist-flyer and affable gentleman—and were soon airborne in his orange and black Cessna 180 with most of our gear aboard.

After arriving, the first item on the project agenda was the erection of the gable framework; the second, the raising and installation of the rafters. As I held a short half-log vertically on top of the log-above-the-plate for Gil to toenail, I found myself questioning the gable design. The half-log seemed so unsupported, like a straw in the wind. However, by the time the diagonals were fixed and the bracing was in place, there seemed to be sufficient strength to bear the rafters.

The hoisting and securing of the first six rafters proceeded smoothly. It was the seventh one, the apex rafter, that gave us the trouble. We had to struggle to get it high enough to ease down into the notched tops of the two high and middle verticals at either end. At the north end, I actually used my hard-hatted head to force this reluctant rafter end up and into the notch. Then, so that it would overhang by three feet at each end of the roof, the rafter had to be advanced northward, something the hoist system couldn't do.

"What do we do now?" I asked.

"I don't know what to do!" Gil replied loudly, momentarily stumped and exasperated.

Gil's outburst recharged his battery, and he hit upon the idea of using the come-along to move this obstinate apex rafter. Within ten minutes, we had the rafter in position. Here's to the humble come-along!

And to the wearing of hard hats. I used to think that hard-hat wearing was overdone, that it was made compulsory by overzealous safety officials. I have since revised that ignorant opinion. I

*Gil splitting cedar shakes for
the roof and gables*

Milling spruce roof boards

Applying roof boards

*The last milled roof board—
the trophy one*

*The shoreline—old cabin, summer house,
and new house*

Early snow on Double-H mountain in October

The new house, almost completed

Inside the new house

Philipp and Martin walking down Christian River en route to Mitchell Lake

now wear my hard hat (formerly son Tom's) regularly when working. Sometimes I have to be reminded to take it off at supper.

On to roof-board milling! We calculated that we needed approximately a hundred boards, each fifteen feet long, seven to twelve inches wide, and one inch thick. We felled four tall spruces close to the site and worked steadily for a week.

Although the Granberg mill rail made setting up easier, there were still problems. We wished we had longer two-headed nails. Where the mill rail was shimmed up at the narrow end it was difficult to pull out the short nails before sawing through without dislodging the mill rail from its shimmed position. On the first de-slabbing, and when the log bulged, we had to cut away the outer, obstructing part with the Stihl saw, then continue the mill cutting. It was mentally demanding for Gil, the setup guy, and it was physically demanding for me, the pusher of the mill. We frequently encouraged each other.

"This is going to make a much better roof in strength and appearance than a plywood one," Gil declared.

"Yeah, and we know whose idea it was to use an Alaska mill," I chortled.

One day we agreed to switch the fishing to the morning and the work to the afternoon. The early jaunt down to Dolly Creek netted us nine rainbow. The post-lunch work effort, however, was nearly disastrous.

It was after 6 p.m., and I was gambling with an unsteady prop-up. As I was slicing the last board from a section of log, the log rolled off the prop-up, I jumped out of the way, the mill-and-saw hit the ground, and the saw's motor stopped. After restoring the prop-up and the milling position, I couldn't start the saw.

"I've wrecked it, I've wrecked it," I moaned.

"Maybe the emergency brake was kicked on," Gil offered, a couple of times.

I guess I didn't hear him. I was sure that the chain had

derailed from the sprocket, and I was trying in vain to get the cover off the sprocket housing. It was dusk by this time, and Gil was holding a flashlight for me. Then it finally clicked: The release for the cover wouldn't operate until the brake was reset. I finally drew a deep breath, regained my senses, reassembled the saw, started it, and resumed work with a fully functioning saw.

At 2 p.m., Saturday, September 22, 1990, we placed the last roof board on the stack. This was the one we'd been looking for. Taking the rest of the day off, I launched the canoe for a spot of fishing at the offshore shelf, and Gil opted for sunbathing. On an earlier occasion, I happened to notice the startling whiteness of Gil's legs and impulsively asked, "Are those your bare legs?" He managed a strained laugh at my rudeness, and for the next few days he was self-conscious of his gams, taking every opportunity to suntan. Someday I may learn to curb my tongue.

"Moose!" hollered Gil early one morning.

I ran out to the shore, and there it was: a fairly young buck retreating southward, but stopping every few strides to peer back at me.

The fine weather continued so that we were able to brave a dip in the lake every second or third day, preferably no later than midafternoon. And we continued working. Cutting the three-quarter-inch plywood for the gables was a bit tricky. We had to allow for a window and several rafter ends. But in a day or so, we finished nailing on the plywood and stapling on the tar paper. Then we framed the skylight space.

Gil had started splitting shakes between the setups for the milling. He used an improvised hitter made of a plastic plumbing piece with a "designer-carved" birch handle and a splitter made from truck-spring blade. The tendency of the handle to come loose was exasperating but was remedied with repeated applications of black tape. While I put up and nailed on the roof boards, Gil continued rhythmically to split high-quality shakes.

On the first day that we applied the shakes to the roof, we completed two-thirds of the back roof, thanks mainly to Gil's setting a brisk pace. It was wise to start on the back roof. The front roof would be better with improved workmanship. We had a couple of minor regrets, though. We remembered to double the initial bottom row, but did it uneconomically with full- instead of half-length shakes. Also, we couldn't achieve straight-line rows because of the varying lengths of shakes. My cutting of the cedar logs into twenty-six-inch lengths had been inconsistent.

Gil and I were determined to complete the closing in. Originally scheduled to go out with Gideon on October 13, we arranged to delay our departure by one week. This change magnified my incipient anxiety about running out of everyday supplies. That I had done most of the shopping for this trip contributed to my unease. It didn't help much when, every once in awhile, Gil would report that we were just about out of such-and-such a food item. Of course, that effectively prompted us to knock off work and go fishing to restock the larder.

As we passed the midpoint of the sojourn, my anxiety gnawed increasingly as I thought, we're going to run out of this; we're going to run out of that. I kept this fussing largely to myself, shaking myself crossly and thinking, so we run out, can't do a thing about it, we will just have to do without or improvise; so cut it out—stop stewing.

By the first week of October, the weather had deteriorated. On October 3, rain stopped us from going on with shaking the front roof. So we switched to installing windows (mainly Gil) and to cutting and installing upper wall logs (mainly me). At noon, Gideon arrived at the Executive Lodge with Ben Rauman and his son Hans. The Raumans expected to stay until just before freeze-up to finish a building project. Ben seemed pleased with the fly-fishing outfit we presented to him as thanks for all his help. He also seemed to be impressed with our progress on the house.

Neither Gil nor I voiced it, but I think we each found comfort in having others within hailing distance. When Ben and Hans invited us over for a movie that evening, I responded with, "Sure, and tomorrow night you come to our place for the live show."

But they weren't fooling. The last Americans to visit the Executive Lodge had left a VCR and five movies. That night we enjoyed Michael Caine in *Blame It on Rio*. On the way home, we were both disoriented. Had we just emerged from a Calgary theater or were we really at Mitchell Lake? We agreed not to report to our womenfolk this addition to Mitchell life because it would diminish the macho image.

In the early morning of October 4, a wet snow fell, leaving a coating of white under a dark sky. The weather almost cleared about midafternoon, but not quite. We put on another layer of clothing and plodded on with the project.

Gil completed the window installation while I bleached the mildew-blackened inner gable verticals with Javex. He then built an exceptionally fine front door, while I boated additional cedar chunks (allocated to us by Ben) from the south shore to our site. Then I began to split shakes from the cedar.

Gil was having trouble with cold feet, and I tried to persuade him to warm his socks above the stove before putting them on, a procedure vital to my well-being. Supplying the stove with firewood was now my first priority each day.

As the cold continued and our pick-up date approached, we encouraged each other: "Yes! With over two weeks left, we will surely get a break in the bad weather to finish putting shakes on the front roof. A day would do it."

As our food supply diminished, especially the cookies and Stoned Wheat Thins, I got more and more hollow-legged. I was always hungry. Ben, in his incredibly sensitive manner, slipped us each a chocolate bar every evening. Never have I received a gift more gratefully.

On the way home from viewing a second movie at the Executive Lodge "theater" (and enjoying delicious cornbread that Hans had made), we looked across the lake to the massive mountain west of the Christian valley. Its two and a half peaks were cloaked in snow and brilliantly illuminated by the full moon, inspiring Gil to promise that he would look into nighttime photography.

October 10 was my forty-first wedding anniversary. What a woman Dora is! She has been a rock through forty interesting and trying years—and I know I have been trying more often than interesting. She has been the vital contributor to my continuing good health and pleasure in this actively retired phase of my life, agreeing that Mitchell is a prime part of the formula. I appreciate her more today than ever before.

We did complete the closing-in of the new house before flying out on October 19. It took a few hundred more shakes, harvested with expert help from Ben and Hans and split deftly by Gil. To finish the front roof, I had to clear off crusty snow and keep the safety rope attached to my middle. But we got the roof and everthing else done. We finished shaking the two gables, installed and flashed the skylight, hammered on reddish brown mottled spruce slabs inside and out to cover gaps, made anti-bear shutters, and cleaned up our debris.

Late on one of the last afternoons, a rare bit of sun illuminated our end of the lake with a triangular reflection on the water a few yards out. I sat on the deck of the new house enjoying this brief burst of glorious sunshine along with a delicious sense of accomplishment. I thought about the wolf we had heard howling a couple of times to the north of us. Its howl had been both forlorn and strident, chilling our nerves with its reverberation. I'm not keen on installing a gas generator, whose ongoing drone would muffle the sounds of nature. It's enough that on too many days we desecrate our haven here with the obscene screaming of a chain saw. I want to be able, always, to hear the wolf's howl.

CHAPTER FOURTEEN

Is the Future of the Wilderness Assured?

In July 1991, I spent two weeks enjoying life in the new Mitchell Lake house by myself. I got on with chinking, insulating, trimming windows, and building furniture and counters.

Patrick Donovan had visited earlier that summer; his bread baking made his visit truly memorable. Before Patrick flew out, I anticipated being entirely alone at the lake until Gil arrived with his family at the end of the month. It made me a little anxious. But then Don Carter arrived in his Cessna with Ben and Hans Rauman. As independent as I like to think I am, I had to admit I was considerably relieved to have more company.

One day Ben reported seeing two hikers camped at the site of an old trapper's cabin across the lake. That night I saw their campfire. Mighty curious, I decided to pass their camp the next evening as I returned from fishing at Twin Creek. Approaching in my boat, I could see two young men on the shore.

"Hello!" I called out. "Could you use a couple of trout for supper?"

"Yes, thank you," one replied with a pleasant smile. "We just have two small ones."

They were squatting on a dock that they had improvised by tying poles together, and one of them had a jig-fishing rig in hand.

In their early twenties, they were both slightly built, but the quantity of their equipment indicated that they were in very good physical shape for backpacking.

Martin Heller and Philipp Huettel introduced themselves and told me they were from Germany. They confirmed my guess that they had backpacked down from Christian Lake. In recounting their jaunt in remarkably good English, they emphasized that it had taken them eight long hours and that when the trail had disappeared, they had had to hike down a long stretch of the river. This didn't surprise me. I remembered the experience Gil and I had had attempting that same hike.

Flown in to Christian Lake, Martin and Philipp had cached food and then climbed the two-and-a-half-peaked mountain immediately west of the Christian Valley. Since both of their surnames start with H, they named the mountain the Double-H. Stormy weather had often made it difficult for them to find dry firewood. Caught in a snowstorm at the top, they had spent hours cooped up in their tent trying to keep dry and warm. But they were still smiling and determined to soldier on.

I invited Martin and Philipp to hike over to our corner. Not expecting to find any life at Mitchell Lake, they were curious about us, the chain saw noise, and Don Carter's frequently flying in and out. They accepted the invitation, arriving in the rain two afternoons later.

On arrival, they presented me with a package of blueberries picked the day before. I gave them warm pork and beans, hot tea, and cookies. When they asked repeatedly what they could do for me, I finally suggested they could clear the beach on another day, if they wished. A little later, Ben joined us and offered to boat the two young men back to their camp.

They returned the next day and did a fine job of clearing the driftwood along our beach, from the old house to the new. And they supplied lunch. Over an outdoor fire, they cooked a tasty, filling, German version of bannock. We sat on the picnic bench, me in the middle, and talked of many things.

We talked about sports. Martin, a footballer, knew a fair bit about hockey, including the Stanley Cup series. And they updated me on Wimbledon results. We touched briefly on twentieth-century European history, but Philipp's number-one subject—the wilderness—was the topic the three of us most readily shared an interest in. When Philipp asked about books, I recommended Michener's *Journey* and Berton's *The Arctic Grail.*

The two young men's hike down from Christian Lake was only one leg of a five-week, heavy-pack itinerary. They planned to spend a few days at Mitchell Lake, return to Christian Lake to restock food, and then set out on an exploration of Niagara Creek.

Being in a position to offer friendship to people like Martin and Philipp enhances this character-building experience for me. I am not alone in my need for retreating and recharging. The enthusiasm and courage of these two young men confirm the value of Mitchell Lake and emphasize the need to support the sustained and extended protection of our wilderness. If it is worthwhile for the Philipps and Martins to travel here from Europe to test themselves, then this wilderness must be preserved for our own children and other sons and daughters in a shrinking world.